Namesake

When God Rewrites Your Story

A Bible Study by
Jessica LaGrone

ABINGDON PRESS

Nashville

NAMESAKE: WHEN GOD REWRITES YOUR STORY

Copyright © 2013 Abingdon Women

This book is printed on acid-free paper.

ISBN 978-1-4267-6187-4

18 19 20 21 22—10 9 8 7 6 5 4 3

MANUFACTURED IN THE UNITED STATES OF AMERICA

Dedication

To the ones who named me: Mom and Dad, thank you for writing such a beautiful introduction for my story. If I ever forget to tell you how grateful I am—you have it here in writing!

To the ones whom I have named: Andrew James and Katherine Juliet, I pray your stories will be filled with richest moments of closeness to Jesus. When there is pain, may He write comfort. When there is joy, be sure to write gratitude. Most of all, know that He who began a good story for you will be faithful to complete it.

Contents

Introduction

In the classroom I answered to the name of Jessica, but as soon as we hit the playground for recess I had an alter ego, a code name. I was Crystal.

The playground was a place of transformation. We each took on new identities in our pretend games, telling our friends to call us by new names we imagined to be more adventurous-sounding than our own. As Crystal I was beautiful and super strong. I had long, flowing hair (in reality I sported a bowl cut for most of elementary school) and a pretend karate chop that was fierce. I could entertain at the most elegant tea party or run after bad guys and beat them up, just like in *Charlie's Angels*.

The picture of whom I wanted so badly to be was vastly different from the little girl who always sat in the front row with the other short kids in class pictures. But calling myself by a different name produced a picture in my head that made me feel as strong and beautiful as I imagined.

The identity I created was an imaginary one. But what if there really is a new name, a new identity, for each of us—one that has been dreamed up in the mind of God? What if your future isn't determined just by your best dream for yourself? What if you are becoming God's best dream for you—a dream that, according to Ephesians 3:20, is far better than all we can ask or even imagine? My imaginings and dreams for my life have changed and grown with the years beyond my playground dreams, and I'll bet yours have too. If we can dream big dreams for ourselves, imagine how great God's dreams for us must be!

The time we'll spend together in this study will help you learn more about God's dreams for your life and how He wants to make them reality.

Namesake is intended to help you discover the transformational power of God through the stories of biblical characters who came to know God and whose lives and names were never the same. Over the next six weeks, you will explore the stories of Abraham and Sarah, Jacob, Naomi, Daniel, Peter, and an unnamed woman.

You and a group of friends will see that God wants to be just as intimately involved in *your* stories, offering each of you an identity that shines with the purpose for which you were created—to know Him through His Son, Jesus, and to become more and more like Him, bringing God glory for His name's sake.

In addition to discovering how God works to bring this transformation in our lives, you also will explore how God has revealed Himself to us in Scripture—and how He desires to reveal Himself personally to each and every one of us. He is a God who reveals and transforms. My prayer is that you will come to know Him in a deeper and more personal way as you invite Him to rewrite your own life story, allowing His dreams for you to come true.

Transformation and Revelation

Each week in your reading you'll find the themes of *transformation* and *revelation*. Let's take a closer look at these themes and what they have to do with God's dreams for us.

Transformation is true and remarkable change. It's what happens when something is no longer its old self but becomes something else. All of the people we will encounter in our journey together experienced transformation at God's hands.

God is not only great at creating (from scratch); He's great at transforming. When His creation goes astray, He doesn't walk away or shake His head in disgust. He rolls up His sleeves and gets down to the business of transformation. He nudges, whispers, shouts, pulls, and prompts until we get the picture of what He desires for us to become. And then He gently helps us get there.

Through transformation God declares: "Behold, I am making all things new" (Revelation 21:5 NASB).

Revelation is more than just the name of the last book of the Bible. Revelation is the noun that happens when you reveal something. Revelation is what God does from beginning to end in Scripture. He reveals Himself and His character to His people again and again, ultimately coming to us in human form through Jesus so that we might truly know Him and how He feels about us.

When we know who He is, our understanding of who we are and what we are about shifts dramatically. All true transformation starts with revelation, not about ourselves, but about the One who has the power to show us who we are and change us into whom we are called to be.

Through revelation God declares: "I AM WHO I AM" (Exodus 3:14).

Throughout our study we'll be bouncing back and forth between the questions "Who is God?" and "Who is God calling me to become?" These questions are so related that the attempt to answer one will always lead us to ask the other. The six stories from the Bible we will study together will help illustrate six different times that God stepped into lives that needed changing and announced His presence and power with grace and truth.

I hope you'll be listening for the echoes of your own story each week. Exploring our identities is a lifelong process. At every stage and in every experience of life we are led to ask again: "Who is God, and who is He calling me to become?"

Getting Started

For each week of our study there are five readings. The first four explore the theme of transformation found in the featured Bible story, and the last one focuses on the theme of God's revelation of Himself. Each of these readings includes the following segments:

Read God's Word	A portion of the Bible story for the week, occasionally with other Scripture readings.
Reflect and Respond	A guided reflection and study of the Scripture with space for recording your responses. (Boldface type indicates write-in-the-book questions or activities.)
Pray About It	A prayer suggestion and/or sample prayer to guide you into a personal time of prayer.
Act on It	Ideas to help you act on what you have read.

You will be able to complete each reading in about 20–30 minutes. (You will need a pen or pencil and your Bible.) Completing these readings each week will help to prepare you for the discussion and activities of the group session.

Once a week you will gather with your group to watch a video in which I share additional insights into the stories and their application in our lives. I encourage you to discuss what you're learning and to share how God is working to transform your own stories. You will find that sharing with one another will enable you to recognize God's activity in your lives even more clearly and help you to encourage and pray for one another.

Before you begin this journey, give God permission to work on your heart and your life. Offer yourself to Him and express your desire to live into the new story He is writing for you. May God richly bless you as you study His Word and discover the wonderful things that happen when God rewrites your story!

Blessings,

Jessica La Grone

Week 1
Abraham and Sarah

Every Name Tells a Story: Little Mike

A name can function as a password, a key that allows you access to its owner. When I visit people in the hospital, that key can unlock doors or leave me standing out in the cold.

When I walk into a hospital, the first person I meet is usually the receptionist at the information desk. My response to the question "Can I help you?" is generally to offer a name. "I'm here to visit Mike Drummond," I said on a recent hospital visit. The woman paused, glanced at her computer screen, and smiled at me: "I'm sorry, we don't have a patient here by that name."

I'm used to this game. Because of privacy laws, hospitals won't give access to the room number of a patient unless the visitor knows the exact legal name entered in the records. So I tried again. "OK, how about *Michael* Drummond?" Same pause, back to the computer, and then another smiling response: "There's no one admitted in this hospital by that name." By this time I was beginning to get frustrated, but a few well-placed cell phone inquiries to mutual friends brought me back to the desk with my password ready: "*Thomas* Drummond!" I said triumphantly. Success! This time I was rewarded with a room number and directions to the elevators.

Mike lay in his hospital bed looking a bit weak but cheerful. Even cancer couldn't put a damper on his hearty personality. After asking about how he was feeling and when he might get to go home, I got to the question stirring my curiosity: "Mike, how is it that I've known you all this time and had no idea your name is really Thomas?" The story he shared was worth the trip *and* the delay in the lobby.

Thomas Philip Drummond Jr. was the first son to a wonderful mother and father. His dad, Tom, was proud to share his name with his little boy. The family lived in Illinois when he arrived but soon packed up and moved back home to be close to his mother's family. There was one little wrinkle. Little Thomas Jr.'s aunts protested because this first-born grandson wasn't named after their father, his grandfather on his mother's side. Thomas Jr.'s parents insisted he keep the name he had received on his birth certificate, but the aunts would hear none of it. They began calling him after his grandfather anyway—Francis Marion Jennings, who went by Mike because he was too burly a guy to go by either Francis or Marion.

Thomas Jr.'s parents tried to stick to their guns but were overpowered as the whole family insisted on calling him Little Mike. Eventually even his parents gave in, and Little Mike it was. Mike claims that for the first three years of his life he thought his first name was all one word: Littlemike. It was a long time before he discovered his given name wasn't Mike at all.

Mike is honored to share the names of his father and grandfather. They were both honorable men, he says—capable, loving, strong, and family-oriented. He knows he couldn't go wrong being named after two wonderful men. He's proud to be their namesake.

A namesake is usually someone given the name of a predecessor in hopes that he or she will grow up and emulate that person in some way. Parents hope their little girl or boy will adopt his or her namesake's traits as the child is called by that name. Little Mike eventually dropped the "Little" and became just Mike. He hopes that he carries that name in a way that would make his grandfather proud. He also has great hopes and dreams for his own son and namesake, Thomas Philip Drummond III, who goes by Phil.

The word *Christian* bears, at its heart, the name of Christ. When that name is bestowed on us, God hopes and dreams that we will grow to favor His Son, to be like Him in all that we are and do. Becoming Jesus' namesake is a complicated, lifelong process of transformation that begins with the simple act of trusting Him.

Abram and Sarai discovered that the God they encountered had such big dreams for them that their entire lives were about to change, including their names. Their identities were so altered by God that their old names simply didn't fit the persons they were becoming. Their new names became a key to a new life, a password of sorts, given by a God who knew them even better than they knew themselves. As we explore their story this week, we will begin our own journey of change. Who are we? Who is God calling us to become? The answers are in the hands of the One who hopes to become our namesake.

Day 1: What's in a Name?

Read God's Word

¹ The LORD had said to Abram, "Leave your country, your people and your father's household and go to the land I will show you.

² "I will make you into a great nation
*   and I will bless you;*
I will make your name great,
*   and you will be a blessing.*
³ I will bless those who bless you,
*   and whoever curses you I will curse;*
and all peoples on earth
*   will be blessed through you."*

⁴ So Abram went, as the Lord had told him; and Lot went with him. Abram was seventy-five years old when he set out from Haran.

Genesis 12:1-4

Reflect and Respond

I've always been intrigued by the stories behind people's names. When someone is introduced to me by name, I often find myself on a scavenger hunt of questions to find out if it has an anecdote attached to it. Harper—Is that a family name? Boston—Is that city a special place for your family? I'm truly curious about names, but sometimes people look at me as if I'm a little too nosy! Most people love to tell their story. Sometimes they have a clear namesake— someone whose name was passed down to them in hopes they would carry on some characteristic or attribute. Other times parents seem to have chosen a name at random. I've known more than one couple who arrived at the hospital for the birth of their child without knowing what they would write on the birth certificate. One couple even put their list up on the wall of the delivery room and let the medical staff vote!

One set of parents I know used to try out potential names for their unborn children by attaching titles to the end to see how they sounded. Piper Johnson, Attorney at Law. Reginald Johnson, M.D. If the name seemed to fit the dream they had for their child, they would put it on their short list.

Those living in the time when the Bible was written definitely invested a lot of effort and thought when they named their children. Names were given to tell a story. A name could carry in it the story of the circumstances surrounding a birth or the weight of the hopes and dreams a child's parents had for him or her. Introductions by name revealed the character or blessings parents hoped children would embody as they grew. Robert L. Hubbard Jr. puts it this way: "In Israel, names were not just labels of individuality but descriptions of inner character . . . presumed to influence the person's conduct."[1]

Read 1 Samuel 1:1-20. When Samuel is named in verse 20, what idea does his mother try to convey with his naming?

Read Genesis 29:31-35; 30:1-12. In just a word or two, tell what you learn about the reasons given for naming each of these great-grandchildren of Abraham and Sarah:

Reuben

Simeon

Levi

Judah

Dan

Naphtali

Gad

Asher

Abraham and Sarah themselves—named Abram and Sarai at birth—were certainly born to parents trying to tell a story with their children's names.

Baby Abram was given a name that seems odd to us now. Not many of us would look at a tiny newborn, all squinty-eyed with tiny fingernails, and pronounce him "Exalted Father," which is what Abram's name means in Hebrew. To us, it seems strange to gaze at a newborn and call him "Father," but to his parents it represented all of their greatest dreams for him. Abram's parents wanted his

*He took him
outside and said,
"Look up at the
sky and count the
stars—if indeed
you can count
them." Then
he said to him,
"So shall your
offspring be."
Genesis 15:5*

name to tell the story of his future life as one filled with prosperity, and for them that meant growing up to be a father with lots of children.

Without currency or stocks or investments, the measure of permanent wealth in that day was carried in your land and your children. So for baby Abram's parents to wish him a houseful of children who would exalt his name—calling him "Exalted Father"—they were wishing a life of abundance on their baby boy.

On the day of her birth, little Exalted Father's future wife was given a name that's a bit easier for us to understand. Her parents looked at their little bundle of joy and named her "Princess," a term of endearment that we might use as a nickname today. My Little Princess, they said, and that, in Hebrew, came out Sarai.

The Little Princess grew up to marry the Exalted Father, and even more strange than Abram's name must have sounded at birth was the irony that he grew up—grew old, even—and had no children at all. It must have been awkward to introduce himself to someone as Exalted Father and have to answer the inevitable question: *So . . . how many children do you have?* The Exalted Father was the father of none. He and his wife, Sarai, had been married so long that their friends had children—grandchildren even. But Abram and Sarai were childless. And in a culture that placed such high value on the number of offspring one had, this was a devastating blow.

Abram is seventy-five years old when we are first introduced to him and his wife in Scripture (Genesis 12:4). And Sarai—well, let's just say she's no spring chick either. It's to these two card-carrying members of AARP that God appears and begins to make outlandish and epic promises. From their first meeting in Genesis 12 and again in Genesis 17—where, by the way, we learn that Abram is ninety-nine years old—God promises that they will become the parents of many offspring—from a great nation in chapter 12 to many nations in chapter 17. And in chapter 15, God gives Abram a powerful visual to go with this promise.

Read Genesis 15:5. God promised Abram that his offspring would number like _____.

In the time of Abram and Sarai, the stars were an even more meaningful spectacle than they are to us today. Without electricity or pollution, there were even more stars visible in the night sky, and people spent more time gazing at them because there was little else to see after dark. The stars were a beautiful gallery of art, a map to guide their way, and a great and magnificent mystery. When God promised Abram and Sarai offspring as numerous as the stars in Genesis 15:5, it was a mind-blowing prospect.

Read Isaiah 40:26. What does it say about the names of the stars and God's relationship to them?

Read Isaiah 43:1. What does this passage say about our names and God's relationship to us?

What is your reaction to a God who cares about us so intimately and personally? How does it feel to know God formed you and knows you by name?

The promise of God's blessings in Abram and Sarai's lives would be so overwhelming that they would be utterly transformed by God. An encounter with the living God means that one's life will never be the same again. For our aging friends, their very identities would be so altered that it would be like two new persons had emerged. Everything would be different.

Even their names would have to be changed.

God had plans for Abram and Sarai that were far beyond anything they dreamed of. What do these verses say about the plans God has for us?

Jeremiah 29:11

Ephesians 3:20

"For I know the plans I have for you," declares the LORD, "plans to prosper you and not to harm you, plans to give you hope and a future."
Jeremiah 29:11

When your parents chose your name, they likely had a dream in mind. That name had a ring to it when they first spoke it over you—the ring of their hopes and longings for the kind of life they wanted to see you live, the kind of person they wanted to see you become. They may have been picturing your namesake when they gave it to you—someone who gave the name a sense of beauty, integrity, or power for them. Eventually, though, that name became truly your own. It became synonymous with you: with your personality and character. When people speak or think of your name, they picture your face, your heart, their memories of your gifts or your spirit, and your temperament.

As powerful as parents' dreams are for their children, God's dreams for us are even more influential. They are the prevailing story spoken over our lives as we grow and become the person God created us to be. Although Abraham and Sarah would forever be connected to the families that named them, they weren't afraid to step out of the path they were expected to follow and into the plans of God. When we begin to ask questions about God's dreams for us, we may find an even greater story than the one we began the day the ink dried on our birth

certificates. The God who gives new birth always has new plans for us, plans for a journey beyond anything we ever dared to dream.

Pray About It

Ask God to open your heart to the lessons He has to teach you in this study. What are you hoping to learn or gain? Share with Him your expectations, needs, and apprehensions in prayer.

Act on It

- **Does your name tell a story? Do you know the reasons your parents gave you the name that they did? Write a brief description here:**

- **Look up your name in a baby name book or on a baby name website, and write the meaning here:**

- **Look up the names of other family members and write the meanings here:**

- **Names are great conversation starters. Just for fun, ask some friends this week if there is a story behind their name. And if you are around people wearing nametags or introducing themselves by name, ask them where their names originated. Record any interesting findings here:**

Day 2: Small Changes, Big Impact

Read God's Word

¹ *When Abram was ninety-nine years old, the LORD appeared to him and said, "I am God Almighty; walk before me and be blameless.* ² *I will confirm my covenant between me and you and will greatly increase your numbers."*

³ *Abram fell facedown, and God said to him,* ⁴ *"As for me, this is my covenant with you: You will be the father of many nations.* ⁵ *No longer will you be called Abram; your name will be Abraham, for I have made you a father of many nations. . . . "*

¹⁵ *God also said to Abraham, "As for Sarai your wife, you are no longer to call her Sarai; her name will be Sarah.* ¹⁶ *I will bless her and will surely give you a son by her. I will bless her so that she will be the mother of nations; kings of peoples will come from her."*

¹⁷ *Abraham fell facedown; he laughed and said to himself, "Will a son be born to a man a hundred years old? Will Sarah bear a child at the age of ninety?"* ¹⁸ *And Abraham said to God, "If only Ishmael might live under your blessing!"*

¹⁹ *Then God said, "Yes, but your wife Sarah will bear you a son, and you will call him Isaac. I will establish my covenant with him as an everlasting covenant for his descendants after him.* ²⁰ *And as for Ishmael, I have heard you: I will surely bless him; I will make him fruitful and will greatly increase his numbers. He will be the father of twelve rulers, and I will make him into a great nation.* ²¹ *But my covenant I will establish with Isaac, whom Sarah will bear to you by this time next year."* ²² *When he had finished speaking with Abraham, God went up from him.*

Genesis 17:1-5, 15-22

Reflect and Respond

Jeff was one of my favorite speakers to invite to special events for teenagers during the years when I was a youth minister. He always held their attention, and he always had them crying by the end—one of the unspoken standards for success in youth ministry. Jeff's powerful testimony began in his own teenage years, when he had been defiant and wild, rejecting his parents' Christian views and filling his life with parties, alcohol, and rebellion. At the pinnacle of his story, Jeff left a party under the influence of alcohol and tried to drive home. When his best friend stood in his way, intending to stop him from driving drunk, Jeff didn't see him in his rearview mirror and accidentally backed over his friend, killing

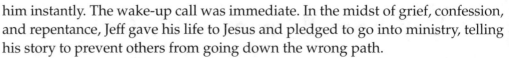

him instantly. The wake-up call was immediate. In the midst of grief, confession, and repentance, Jeff gave his life to Jesus and pledged to go into ministry, telling his story to prevent others from going down the wrong path.

Our teens loved the drama of Jeff's testimony and the real transformation they saw in him. Each time he told his story, a handful of them realized they were on the same path of rebellion and made a dramatic turn with their own lives.

But then there were the rest of the kids—regular churchgoers living less than dramatic lives. Many of them had already given their lives to Christ. Most could not identify with the remarkable circumstances of Jeff's life. When asked to tell about how God was working in their lives, some of them lamented, "I don't really have a testimony. God hasn't done much in my life compared to Jeff." They didn't realize that they were being daily transformed in little ways, or that it was important to expect God's help with the smallest things. Turning their temptations toward greed, lust, selfishness, and materialism (to name a few) over to God, bit by bit, was forming a dramatically different future for them. They were becoming new and different people, but sometimes the alterations were almost too small to see.

In light of the big changes God wanted to make in Abram and Sarai's lives, the changes in their names seem so small. In fact, it was just one Hebrew letter each. But when God makes changes, the tiniest adjustment can communicate big things for us, our futures, and those whose lives we will impact.

Abram and Sarai each received the same letter as an addition to their names. In Hebrew the letter is called "Hey" (similar to our "H"). Abram became Abraham and Sarai became Sarah.

In Hebrew, letters have significance beyond just a pronounced sound. Each character of the Hebrew alphabet is infused with meaning. The letter Hey, for example, also signifies the number five, since it's the fifth letter of the Hebrew alphabet. Hey sometimes represents the divine breath, revelation, and light. In some Jewish teachings, Hey is a picture of the presence of God within the human heart. Adding Hey at the very end of a Hebrew noun gives the word a feminine character, which can metaphorically mean the word has become "fruitful" or reproductive.

What did the addition of that one letter mean to Abraham and Sarah? It shifted the meaning of their names to fit God's plan for their future. Abram, which means "The Exalted Father," was now Abraham, which means "The Father of Many Nations."

"As for me, this is my covenant with you: You will be the father of many nations. No longer will you be called Abram; your name will be Abraham, for I have made you a father of many nations. I will make you very fruitful; I will make nations of you, and kings will come from you."

Genesis 17:4-6

The slight alteration in the spelling of Sarai's name to Sarah changed the meaning from "Little Princess" to an actual royal title. Sarah means "A True Princess," one who will be the mother of kings and princes.

God also said to Abraham, "As for Sarai your wife, you are no longer to call her Sarai; her name will be Sarah. I will bless her and will surely give you a son by her. I will bless her so that she will be the mother of nations; kings of peoples will come from her."

Genesis 17:15-16

Hearing their new names spoken by God must have been an awesome moment, one where God painted a clear picture of the future He had in mind for them. That little letter revealed a God who wanted to dwell in their hearts, making His presence as accessible as their next breath, as well as the new life awaiting them—a life that was fruitful and reproductive, infused with hope for a family they had dreamed of and a God who would surround and bless them.

Mark the significance of this simple yet profound name change for Abraham and Sarah. Record the meaning of each name in the chart below.

Old Name	Meaning	New Name	Meaning
Abram		Abraham	
Sarai		Sarah	

How do you think these name changes might have affected Abraham and Sarah?

Too often we underestimate the value of small changes God makes in our lives. What looks like one little letter to us meant the world to Abraham and Sarah. Dramatic testimonies are inspiring, but if we miss the small changes God is making, we will miss the big picture He's painting for a big future.

When I think about the changes God wants to make in our lives, I think of Nicodemus. I've always been fascinated by the story of Nicodemus, a man who had to sneak around to meet with Jesus in the middle of the night. He brings to mind what my parents would tell me when they reminded me of my curfew as

"God works powerfully, but for the most part gently and gradually." —John Newton, writer of the lyrics to "Amazing Grace"

19

a teenager: "Nothing good happens after midnight!" Nicodemus intrigues me because the mysterious encounter he has after dark turned out to be something good after all—something that changed his entire life.

Nicodemus's story is told in John 3:1-21. Nicodemus was a Pharisee, a religious leader in his day, known for living life on the "up and up." No sneaking around for him! But because the Pharisees were a group of Jesus' most ardent critics and enemies, Nicodemus snuck in to talk to Jesus at night. He wanted to hide his interest in Jesus and his teaching, an interest that would have been looked on unfavorably by the other Pharisees and their followers.

Read John 3. Does Nicodemus profess faith in Jesus' words? Do we know from this passage about changes that Nicodemus felt internally or made in his life?

Now read John 19:38-42. What do we find Nicodemus doing here in the light of day, in the middle of a crowd?

What do you think brought about the changes we see in Nicodemus from chapter 3 to chapter 19—changes that led Nicodemus to make a public statement with his actions toward Jesus?

Nicodemus's faith developed in a way that many Christians can identify with. First, he was curious about Jesus but hesitant to do anything about it. He probably watched believers around him carefully, wondering what made their lives so different from the rule-bound Pharisees he spent his time with. When he could no longer contain his curiosity, he began to talk privately to Jesus. His faith was hidden from the light of day for a while so that no one could question or make fun of him. Then he finally went public with his convictions. The crucifixion of Jesus meant that Nicodemus couldn't contain or hide his faith any longer. He wanted to do something about it.

Going public with our faith involves a great deal more than attending church or wearing a Christian T-shirt. It means showing the characteristics of Christ in our lives that match the change going on in our hearts. Public faith affects the way we treat others, the way we handle anger or disappointment, and the way we choose to sacrifice for the good of others.

The outward traits of someone who has been transformed by God are often called the fruit of the Spirit. These nine traits may seem like small characteristics, but when they grow in a life with God's help, they shine powerfully. The fruit of the Spirit grows as you live your life surrendered to God's Holy Spirit.

Read Galatians 5:22-23 and list the fruit of the Spirit below.

1. _____

2. _____

3. _____

4. _____

5. _____

6. _____

7. _____

8. _____

9. _____

But the fruit of the Spirit is love, joy, peace, patience, kindness, goodness, faithfulness, gentleness and self-control.
Galatians 5:22-23

Is there one or more of these nine characteristics that is more evident in your life? Circle the characteristics above that you can see growing in you.

Is there a characteristic you would like to be more evident in your life? Put a checkmark beside it.

Are there people who come to mind whose lives are like living produce sections, growing the fruit of the Spirit in obvious ways? Write their name or initials next to the characteristics that you see evident in them.

I love powerful stories of people whose lives were changed by Jesus in a big way. A friend of mine was lost in addiction, hit rock bottom, and found forgiveness and sobriety. A woman I know was angry and bitter, hurting those around her without a second thought. When she met Jesus, her family and coworkers saw an instant, dramatic change in her. One man lived a life shaped by greed, ignoring his close relationships so he could work to attain more and more material things. When God changed his heart, he became one of the most generous people I know.

But for every person with a big testimony, marked with a clear and instantaneous before and after story, I know dozens who can testify to tiny, incremental change. Change like this is almost imperceptible if you try to catch it happening, like trying to watch a tendril of ivy wind its way up a brick wall. Stare at it and it seems never to change. Look at it every few days, or every few weeks, and you'll see its progress. Check on it once a year and you'll see it take over the whole wall. I think God designed it this way. He knew we would need constant reminders, repeated help, and consistent attention to our relationship with Him. If everything changed in an instant, we wouldn't need the help He offers on a daily, hourly, minute-by-minute basis. With His patient attention, though, the changes in us will become apparent over time. Our faith will bloom.

What are some changes you've experienced over the years with God's help—whether small or large? How are you different now than five to ten years ago?

It takes time to become the persons God wants us to be. I'm thankful to have a lifetime to practice listening for God's voice and following His directions. Abraham and Sarah's story shows us how, over time, little changes add up. And it reveals the heart of a patient God, who never gives up on His dreams for us.

Pray About It

What changes in your own life and character has God helped you to make? Say a prayer of thanksgiving for His help in transforming you.

What changes still need to be made in your own heart and actions? Lift these desired changes to God and place them in His hands. Tell Him that you are open to any changes He wants to make in you.

Read Ephesians 1:6 out loud. Thank God for being willing and able to complete the good work He has already begun in you.

Act on It

- Think of someone who is close to you (family member or friend) in whom you have noticed changes over time—whether small or large. Take a moment today to tell or write this person how proud you are of his or transformation.

- Find the Hebrew equivalent of your name at www.my-hebrew-name.com. (*Note: If you have an unusual name, there may not be an equivalent listed on this site. If you do find a Hebrew name, be sure to click on it to see it spelled out in Hebrew.*)

Day 3: Promises, Promises

Read God's Word

¹ When Abram was ninety-nine years old, the LORD appeared to him and said, "I am God Almighty; walk before me and be blameless. ² I will confirm my covenant between me and you and will greatly increase your numbers."

³ Abram fell facedown, and God said to him, ⁴ "As for me, this is my covenant with you: You will be the father of many nations. ⁵ No longer will you be called Abram; your name will be Abraham, for I have made you a father of many nations. ⁶ I will make you very fruitful; I will make nations of you, and kings will come from you. ⁷ I will establish my covenant as an everlasting covenant between me and you and your descendants after you for the generations to come, to be your God and the God of your descendants after you. ⁸ The whole land of Canaan, where you are now an alien, I will give as an everlasting possession to you and your descendants after you; and I will be their God."

Genesis 17:1-8

Reflect and Respond

At nine years old I was already a bit jaded. I understood that television commercials promised things their products would never be able to deliver. I felt sure that it was false advertising when my grandmother guaranteed that eating all my vegetables would make me grow up to have big muscles. And I knew that grownups didn't always keep their promises. By the end of elementary school I had witnessed my own parents' divorce and their remarriages to other people that were already beginning to crumble. Stepparents, stepbrothers and stepsisters, and step-grandparents were impermanent stars in confused and fading family constellations. People came into my life making vows to one another and to me, but I was learning quickly that they often didn't hold up their end of those promises. Before I ever hit puberty I learned to look with caution when a grownup made a promise to stay forever.

My ninth year was also the summer that I stood on a hillside at a Christian camp in the Texas hill country, contemplating the promises of God. My counselors taught me about Jesus' love for me, about His invitation to a lifelong, life-changing relationship, and about His faithfulness. It was the faithfulness part I questioned. If grownups couldn't keep their promises to each other or to me, how could I trust this God with my heart? How did I know He would keep His word? Would God love me forever, or would He bail when things got tough? Somehow during that week the hardness of my little third-grade heart began to melt. I wanted so badly for someone to love me and stay forever. So I took a chance and said yes to Jesus.

Read the following Scripture passages. What does each say about God's promises?

Numbers 23:19

Joshua 23:14

John 14:1-2

2 Peter 3:9

Abraham and Sarah didn't have much experience with a God who made promises and kept them. The religion of their families had been one of polytheism—the belief in many gods. In this practice, their families would've had a shrine or altar with multiple idols dedicated to different gods. When they wanted something, they would pick an idol that specialized in that area (for example, a god or goddess of fertility, war, healing, or harvest) and make sacrifices and promises to win that god's approval and favor. Worshipping at the family altar was often about what they wanted and how to manipulate their false gods to get it, rather than responding to a God who wanted something from them.

This God, however, was clearly different than any they had ever heard of before. He sought them out and made contact instead of waiting for them to come to Him. He made promises to them that were about His will instead of them making promises and sacrifices to Him in hopes that He would do their will. Most of all, He was real. And powerful. And loving. And more than capable of fulfilling every promise that He made.

Reread today's Scripture passage (p. 23) and circle each time that God says, "I will." How many times did you find "I will" in these verses?

"Do not let your hearts be troubled. Trust in God; trust also in me. In my Father's house are many rooms; if it were not so, I would have told you. I am going there to prepare a place for you."
John 14:1-2

Is this phrase in first, second, or third person?

Is this phrase in past, present, or future tense?

What conclusion can you make based on these answers?

Sandra Richter sums up the promises God makes to His people in three words: people, place, and presence.[2]

First, God promised them a people.

Reread Genesis 17:6, 15-16 and fill in the blanks below:

"I will make you very _____; I will make _____ of you, and kings will come from you."

Genesis 17:6 (NIV)

"As for Sarai your wife, . . . I will bless her and will surely give you a son by her. I will bless her so that she will be the mother of _____; kings of _____ will come from her."

Genesis 17:15-16 (NIV)

This promise might be the one that caught Abraham and Sarah's attention because it addressed a long-awaited desire of their hearts: a family. God promised not only a little bundle they could call their own but also a family that would be as plentiful as the stars in the heavens or the grains of sand on the shore. This would result not just in a little nuclear family but also in a people, one that would be blessed by God and share His blessings with the world. The "people" promised here were the beginning of a family line. God's chosen people. God promised that He would bring blessings to Abraham's offspring.

Read Galatians 3:26-29 and Romans 9:8. Who is included now in this list of Abraham's descendants?

What does it mean to be part of this line?

Read John 1:12-13, 1 John 3:1-2, and Romans 8:15-17. Describe what it means personally to know you're part of this covenant of amazing promises.

The second thing God promised them was a place—a land that would hold all these future nations, a place they could call home for generations to come.

Reread Genesis 17:8 and fill in the blanks below:

"The whole _____ of _____, where you are now an alien, I will give as an everlasting possession to you and your descendants after you." **(NIV)**

It would be a land that would be amazingly beautiful and fruitful and belong to their family. Remember that permanent wealth wasn't determined by currency in the bank but by many children and ownership of land to pass down through the generations. These two promises alone were the equivalent of winning the lottery many times over.

Third, and best of all, God promised them a presence—His presence.

Reread Genesis 17:7-8 and fill in the blanks below:

"I will establish my covenant as an everlasting covenant between me and you and your descendants after you for the generations to come, to be _____ _____ and the God of your descendants after you. . . . I will be _____ _____." **(NIV)**

He promised to be with them and to be their God—to love and take care of them.

God promised Abraham and Sarah three things: the two greatest desires of their hearts—people and place—and a third thing they hadn't even imagined they could desire, because the presence of a God who loved and cared and guided them through life was unheard of. The greatest promise of all was that He would be with them, establishing a covenant to be their God and the God of their descendants. This third promise was worth more than the others combined—God's presence with them. The greatest promise of all is God's presence, His commitment to walk with us as His children.

What do you learn from the following verses about God's presence?

Psalm 16:11

Psalm 41:12

Acts 17:28

While Abraham and Sarah were used to making their own promises to idols that were false and powerless, they suddenly found themselves in the presence of the God who was powerful and true—who took ownership of the outcome and made clear that He would be the power behind these great works by over and over again using the words "I will" to describe His intentions to fulfill this new covenant.

This God is clearly not one to be manipulated and controlled like an idol but is the One in control. The promises made are to fulfill His will and purpose. As for an itinerary or timeline, God is not exact on that point. He just points to a time in the future and says, "I will." I'm sure Abraham and Sarah were thrilled at the prospect of such great gifts arriving in their lives, while also wishing for a little more detail about how and when they would arrive! I can identify. I often wish God would spell out details about my future instead of expecting me to trust Him.

Letting God be in control is a hard thing, but the fulfillment of His promises is so much better than looking to our own devices or fruitlessly worshipping the false gods of this world to try to get our desires met in our own timing. God's continual promise "I will" means that the responsibility and power for our lives lies in His hands, not our own.

If you'll look back closely at your own story, I'm sure you'll find it is marked by so many gifts that have already arrived: people who have brought you laughter, places that you've treasured, and most of all a presence—His presence.

How has God brought blessings into your life in the following three categories?

1. People who've brought joy to your life:

2. Places you've treasured:

3. The presence of God with you in good times and bad:

> *"For in him we live and move and have our being." As some of your own poets have said, "We are his offspring."* Acts 17:28

If you've ever wondered who will love you unconditionally, who will walk beside you and never leave you, who will give you a place to belong with a people of faith, or who will offer His presence when you need it most, listen to the echo of these words in Genesis 17: *I will. I will. I will.* God doesn't take these promises lightly, and neither should we. Abraham and Sarah discovered that God could and would always keep His promises. I'm so thankful that I turned my nine-year-old heart over to Him. No matter my actions or behavior, He has been faithful in loving me ever since. And He always will. He will do the same for you.

Pray About It

Take a moment to thank God for the blessings in your life of people, place, and presence.

Now look to your future. What are the circumstances or relationships that concern you? Where do you need to trust God's provision? Say a prayer, placing your concerns in God's hands and asking Him to handle them. Believe God's promise: "I will."

Act on It

- Think back on your own journey of faith with Christ. Who are the people God has placed in your path who have made an impact in your life? Offer a prayer of thanksgiving for each of these "gifts" God has blessed you with. If you feel led, call or send a "thank you" note to each one.

- Make a conscious decision this week to look for signs of God's presence around you. Keep a small notebook or file on your computer or phone where you can record the ways you sensed or saw God at work around you. Share these with your group.

Day 4: Waiting on God

Read God's Word

¹ The LORD appeared to Abraham near the great trees of Mamre while he was sitting at the entrance to his tent in the heat of the day. ² Abraham looked up and saw three men standing nearby. When he saw them, he hurried from the entrance of his tent to meet them and bowed low to the ground.

³ He said, "If I have found favor in your eyes, my lord, do not pass your servant by. ⁴ Let a little water be brought, and then you may all wash your feet and rest under this tree. ⁵ Let me get you something to eat, so you can be refreshed and then go on your way—now that you have come to your servant."

"Very well," they answered, "do as you say."

⁶ So Abraham hurried into the tent to Sarah. "Quick," he said, "get three seahs of fine flour and knead it and bake some bread."

⁷ Then he ran to the herd and selected a choice, tender calf and gave it to a servant, who hurried to prepare it. ⁸ He then brought some curds and milk and the calf that had been prepared, and set these before them. While they ate, he stood near them under a tree.

⁹ "Where is your wife Sarah?" they asked him.

"There, in the tent, " he said.

¹⁰ Then the LORD said, "I will surely return to you about this time next year, and Sarah your wife will have a son."

Now Sarah was listening at the entrance to the tent, which was behind him. ¹¹ Abraham and Sarah were already old and well advanced in years, and Sarah was past the age of childbearing. ¹² So Sarah laughed to herself as she thought, "After I am worn out and my master is old, will I now have this pleasure?"

¹³ Then the LORD said to Abraham, "Why did Sarah laugh and say, 'Will I really have a child, now that I am old?' ¹⁴ Is anything too hard for the LORD? I will return to you at the appointed time next year and Sarah will have a son."

¹⁵ Sarah was afraid, so she lied and said, "I did not laugh." But he said, "Yes, you did laugh."

God didn't punish her b/c she didn't get it

Genesis 18:1-15

Reflect and Respond

Hurry up and wait! That phrase or something like it may have echoed in Abraham and Sarah's minds. They received awesome promises from God but no timeline about when they would be fulfilled. They learned quickly that trusting this God and His promises meant a lot of waiting, hoping, and praying.

There were a few years when my life felt like one big waiting room. I spent so much time waiting in doctors' offices that I had read and reread the same magazines, studied the fading pictures on their walls, and knew the receptionists' names by heart. My heart's desire was to become a mom, but my body just wasn't cooperating. After a couple of years in the waiting room of my regular ob-gyn, I moved on to the bigger and more expensive waiting room of a specialist, and a lab, and an operating room, and lots of other places where it seemed like all I could do was . . . wait.

It has always seemed strange to me that those who are in the care of a doctor are called "patients." It was so hard to have any patience with a process in which I had no control. As we slowly unraveled the reasons for our struggle with infertility, more and more doctors prescribed treatments and medications and advised that I continue to wait in their care. I may have been their patient, but I didn't feel very patient.

After what seemed like an eternity of trying, the joy of finding out we were expecting our first baby was quickly eclipsed by the devastating news that I had miscarried. That led to more tests, more doctors' visits, and more practice being an impatient patient while I waited for answers and results. When our hearts desire something so deeply that we can't think of or want anything else, the pain of waiting can be excruciating. I had been trusting God with my life since I was a child, but this was the toughest hurdle yet. When things looked and felt worse than ever, did God still have my hopes and dreams on His to-do list? It was hard to face the answer of "wait and see."

Even if it's not for life-changing news or results, waiting is one of the hardest things we do in life. We don't even like the annoyance of waiting in line at the store, or waiting for our food at a restaurant. Learning to wait well is important, because we'll always be waiting for something. Once we have what we've waited for, it seems to lead to waiting for something else. Hunger is a great example. Once we satisfy it, it's only a matter of time before it returns. We can't expect one meal a day to keep us full! Because our lives are filled with waiting, each of us has to make up our mind: Will I be discontent because I don't yet have what I want, or can I find contentment along the way with God's help? What will I learn in my time of waiting? Am I willing to listen for God as I wait?

What are some things you've had to wait for in your life? How did it feel to wait?

Abraham and Sarah's lives were full of waiting for their longing for a child to be fulfilled. Long after they had hoped to be grandparents, they were still waiting for the baby that God had promised twenty-five years earlier. That's what I call a long time to be expecting!

From their perspective it must have seemed that their prayers were getting harder and harder to answer because of their age, but to a God who loves a challenge, the timing was just right. The more difficult something is to make happen, the more God enjoys rolling up His sleeves and impressing the world by doing what only He can accomplish. When God makes the impossible happen, we can't deny that He's the one behind the results.

Read these stories of others in the Bible who waited. What were they waiting for? What do you learn from each of their stories?

Genesis 8:6-12

1 Samuel 1:1-22

Luke 2:25-35

Often we find that something powerful has happened within us while we were waiting. Waiting for the blessing can often be part of the blessing itself, since we have to rely on God in new and unexpected ways.

An old hymn talks about the learning and changing process that can happen in us while we're waiting.

Have thine own way, Lord! Have thine own way!
Thou art the potter; I am the clay.
Mold me and make me after thy will,
while I am waiting, yielded and still.
Adelaide A. Pollard, 1902

Waiting may be one of the few times in life when we are forced to be still long enough for God to do some of His most important work in us, molding us into whom He wants us to become. Waiting is a struggle because we're so used to the illusion that we control our lives by planning and acting on our plans. We believe that we are the ones who make things happen. Waiting strips us of that illusion and forces us to acknowledge the God who is in control and our need for Him.

> Waiting may be one of the few times in life when we are forced to be still long enough for God to do some of His most important work in us.

31

In the Old Testament there are several words that can be translated to the English word *wait*. The most commonly used Hebrew word translated "wait" is *qavah*. It means "to bind together" (by twisting strands, as in making a rope) or to "look patiently," "tarry or wait," "hope, expect, look eagerly."

Look up the following Scriptures about waiting: Psalm 27:14, Psalm 130:5-7, and Isaiah 40:31. All three use the word *qavah* for wait. Choose your favorite and write it below:

I think this word is my favorite of all the Hebrew words that mean "wait," because of the image of binding things together. God used my time of waiting to bind my marriage and other relationships closer together and to bind my heart closer to His than it had ever been. I never would have chosen the path that we went down over those years. The pain of waiting and loss brings a twinge of tenderness in my heart even years later. But I recognize now that my practice being a "patient" actually strengthened my "patience" more than I could have imagined at the time. Those years gave me a deep appreciation for Abraham and Sarah. When I read their story of waiting, I see between the lines their years of discouragement and anguish but also their growth in trust and hope in God. I know all too well the longing they experienced for the gift they wanted to hold in their arms. But I also know they received countless gifts while holding their empty arms out to God.

Read the following verses: Psalm 40:1, Psalm 119:114, Lamentations 3:25, Isaiah 25:9. What can we learn about God as we trust Him in our waiting?

Waiting means to trust that God is good, even when we can't see it in the ways we wanted or expected. Waiting means seeking God's help and comfort in prayer and worship when we can't find it in our material world. Waiting means asking God to change us instead of expecting to change God. Abraham and Sarah had different hearts, a different marriage, and a different outlook on God's promises after twenty-five years of waiting.

How has waiting changed you or your relationship with God?

Trusting in God doesn't mean that our prayers will be instantaneously answered, as if God were some cosmic vending machine ready to dispense our wishes and wants. Instead, it means that our waiting and longing can become a tool that transforms us rather than an obstacle to happiness and fulfillment.

> "I waited patiently for the LORD;
> he turned to me and heard my cry."
> Psalm 40:1

Choosing to trust God's goodness means that we turn our waiting over to Him. When we do, moments when we impatiently thought nothing was happening at all can become some of the most productive, transformational times of our lives.

Pray About It

Psalm 46:10 tells us to "be still, and know that I am God." Spend some time waiting on God in prayer. This isn't time to ask God for anything or even to talk to Him; it's just a time to wait and be quiet. Set aside a time and place where you can be silent. Set a timer for five or ten minutes if it helps. Sit still and quiet the thoughts of your mind. If a thought comes to your mind, let it float away like a leaf floats downstream, and return your mind to quiet.

This is sometimes difficult the first time or the first few times you try it. Our minds naturally have a lot of thoughts rumbling around, and they pop up quickly when we're quiet. The discipline of quieting your mind and sitting still is one that will carry over to other moments in your days. The peace you receive in this waiting time will seep out into the other areas of your life.

Act on It

- Our experience of waiting has changed drastically with the arrival of cell phones. Many people use their "waiting" time in line, in a doctor's office, and even in traffic to make calls or text messages or check their e-mail and Facebook on their phones. This week, take a day where you intentionally wait in "electronic silence." Look around the doctor's office and observe those around you. Start a conversation with those in line at the grocery store. Observe the people and things around you and ask God to teach you something. What can you learn from your waiting time this week?

- Start a waiting journal. Keep a list of the times you wait and how you feel. Where is your attention as you wait for little things? What is your attitude? How about the big things in your life? Look back and remember waiting for life events and how it felt to wait. Write a paragraph praising God for who He is and what He provides while you wait on Him. Look ahead to things you are waiting for now and write about how God is working in your life as you wait.

They were defiant 2 the will of God.

Day 5: Revelation—
To Call on the Name of God

Read God's Word

East = meaning away from God.

[1] *Now the whole world had one language and a common speech.* [2] *As people moved eastward, they found a plain in Shinar and settled there.*

[3] *They said to each other, "Come, let's make bricks and bake them thoroughly." They used brick instead of stone, and tar for mortar.* [4] *Then they said, "Come, let us build ourselves a city, with a tower that reaches to the heavens, so that we may make a name for ourselves; otherwise we will be scattered over the face of the whole earth."*

They were trying 2 build ↑, 2 reach Heaven + do things their way.

[5] *But the LORD came down to see the city and the tower that the people were building.* [6] *The LORD said, "If as one people speaking the same language they have begun to do this, then nothing they plan to do will be impossible for them.* [7] *Come, let us go down and confuse their language so they will not understand each other."*

[8] *So the LORD scattered them from there over all the earth, and they stopped building the city.*

Genesis 11:1-8

They didn't Scatter like God told them so he had 2 Scatter them. But he spared their lives + showed them Grace

[1] *The LORD had said to Abram, "Go from your country, your people and your father's household to the land I will show you.*

[2] *"I will make you into a great nation,*
   and I will bless you;
I will make your name great,
   and you will be a blessing.
[3] *I will bless those who bless you,*
   and whoever curses you I will curse;
and all peoples on earth will be blessed through you."

Bethel - House of God

[4] *So Abram went, as the LORD had told him; and Lot went with him. Abram was seventy-five years old when he set out from Harran.* [5] *He took his wife Sarai, his nephew Lot, all the possessions they had accumulated and the people they had acquired in Harran, and they set out for the land of Canaan, and they arrived there.*

Built an altar Between Bethel + the ruins.

[6] *Abram traveled through the land as far as the site of the great tree of Moreh at Shechem. At that time the Canaanites were in the land.* [7] *The LORD appeared to Abram and said, "To your offspring I will give this land." So he built an altar there to the LORD, who had appeared to him.*

we r 2 Keep moving Hward

[8] *From there he went on toward the hills east of Bethel and pitched his tent, with Bethel on the west and Ai on the east. There he built an altar to the LORD and called on the name of the LORD.*

[9] *Then Abram set out and continued toward the Negev.*

Genesis 12:1-9

Reflect and Respond

There are certain kinds of change I resist with my whole being. I don't like it when friends move away. I would rather sing my heart out to my favorite songs in worship than learn new songs or new styles of music. I don't want to change shampoos because mine went off the market or switch doctors because my insurance says I have to. But there are also certain kinds of change I long for. These usually have to do with me. I want to be different because my life belongs to God. I want to look back and see that I've grown less selfish and more forgiving. I want to be noticeably more like Jesus than I was a year ago, or even more than I was this morning when I woke up. I long to be transformed.

As I mention in the Introduction, the two main themes of Namesake are transformation and revelation. The first four days each week will deal with transformation, learning about the change God has brought about in others' stories and seeking change in our own lives. Revelation, the topic of the last day of each week, will uncover the unchanging identity and character of God, revealed to us in Scripture.

Transformation is a must for believers. Asking questions and learning about how we can change is helpful, but all of our acquired information and introspection would be incomplete if we didn't learn about the character and name of the One who is the reason and power behind our change. True change is found in discovering who God is, how God reveals Himself and His love to us, and how it makes a difference in our own lives. Only when we begin to see His unchanging character do we find ourselves wanting to change to be more like Him. My desire to be transformed would be a confused circling of my own misguided ideas if I didn't have Jesus as a model of heart and actions. Changing ourselves means first learning about the God who provides both the model and the power to change.

From the very beginning of creation we see God revealing Himself to us, sharing aspects of His character and love, and inviting us to learn more in a relationship with Him. God was never required to clue us in to any of this. He could have remained aloof, unknowable. Imagine what a frustrating and hopeless experiment this life would be if we had no knowledge of the God who created us and loves us intimately!

> True change is found in discovering who God is, how God reveals Himself and His love to us, and how it makes a difference in our own lives.

What do the following passages reveal about the nature and name of God?

Proverbs 18:10

Psalm 113:1-3

John 20:31

Despite God's efforts to know and be known by us, we humans quickly begin to see ourselves as the center of the universe instead of the God who belongs there. The first eleven chapters of the Bible are a depiction of how quickly the world goes downhill when we begin to worship our own misguided desires and put ourselves first.

The story starts off in such a beautiful setting, with perfect relationships, a perfect environment, and a God whose presence and love are palpable. Eden is a place where God and human beings know and are known without any barriers. But all of that quickly changes as human choices invite disaster after disaster. The downward spiral culminates in chapter 11 of Genesis, aptly numbered since it is truly about the moral bankruptcy of the world. The collective people of the world gather in chapter 11 and work toward a common, selfish goal.

> *"Come, let us build ourselves a city, with a tower that reaches to the heavens, so that we may make a name for ourselves."*
>
> Genesis 11:4

Notice that their purpose in building the tower was to make a name for themselves.

Lifting up their own name implied that they were trusting in their own strength and striving for their own fame and success. They were physically reaching for godlike status. Anytime we put ourselves first, declaring that we can live without God's help or guidance, we are putting ourselves in the place that belongs to God. And that always spells trouble.

We often refer to the resulting story as the Tower of Babel. The crashing down of the physical tower is mirrored in the chaos of human relationships and communication. The world as they knew it was in shambles. But the very next chapter provides a deep contrast. Abraham and Sarah are builders, too, but while the people of Babel built a tower and lifted up their own name, Abraham and Sarah built an altar and called on the name of the Lord.

Their first encounter with God in chapter 12 has Abraham and Sarah humbled and in awe of the greatest power in the universe. Their response to hearing the life-changing promises that are to come is to build an altar and call on the name of the Lord.

> *The LORD appeared to Abram and said, "To your offspring I will give this land." So he built an altar there to the LORD, who had appeared to him.*
>
> *From there he went on toward the hills east of Bethel and pitched his tent, with Bethel on the west and Ai on the east. There he built an altar to the LORD and called on the name of the LORD.*
>
> Genesis 12:7-8

Building an altar implies both worship and sacrifice. Calling on the name of God means they are beginning to understand that the characteristics at the heart of God are central to the future they are now seeking.

Even more than with other names in Scripture, the use of "name" in reference to God is so much more than a proper noun that can be spelled on paper or spoken aloud. It is a representation of the One who bears that name: of His character, His promises, His strength. When Abram and Sarai call on the name of the Lord, it is about so much more than getting God's attention. They are worshipping and praising God for who He is and also looking forward to His future help in their lives. At the beginning of chapter 12, God approached them. Now they are coming to God, throwing themselves on the mercy of His promises and His strength.

When we call on God's name, we aren't saying, "God, do things my way"; we're saying, "God, in agreement with who You are, with all Your power, Your love, and mercy, I call on Your name—Your character—to act in this situation."

Prayer that calls on God's name is not about hoping that He will come around to see things the way we do or that He will acquiesce to our will and do things our way. When we call on God's name, we are asking God to change our hearts, our character, to be more like His. Not the other way around.

> *You, Lord, are forgiving and good, abounding in love to all who call to you.*
> Psalm 86:5

Look up these other instances in Scripture of people calling on the name of the Lord. What do you learn from each passage?

Psalm 86:5

Romans 10:13

When Jesus teaches the disciples to pray in Matthew 6, how does He teach them to open each prayer? How are they to call on God's name (v. 9)?

Like Abraham and Sarah and the people of Babel, we're builders, too. We're constructing something with each action, decision, and interaction. We get to choose over and over whether to stay stuck in the bankruptcy of chapter 11 or to move with Abraham and Sarah into worshipping a God so great, so beyond our own fragile human existence, that we instinctively know how much we need Him. Do we want to build a tower to ourselves or an altar to God? Whose name will we call on for strength and help?

37

Think of a time when you have called on God's name for a specific purpose or circumstance. How did you see God reveal Himself to you through that situation?

Proverbs 18:10 declares that "The name of the LORD is a strong tower; the righteous run to it and are safe." A life built for our own glory will only crumble into confusion. A life built for the glory of God's name provides a strong tower, a safe place to reflect, to hope, to grow.

When we recognize just how badly we need to change, it's important that we know the God who never changes. His strength provides an unshakeable foundation, a place where we can trust our hearts to the work of a transforming God.

Pray About It

Find a time and place you can pray out loud. Begin your time of prayer by speaking God's name aloud several times. You might say Lord or Jesus or some other name you've heard used for God such as Shepherd, Warrior, Creator, or Comforter. Ask God to teach you more about Himself and how He wants to be part of your life. Let God know that you aren't calling to ask Him to do things your way but, in agreement with who He is, you want to be part of His plan for the world and for your future.

Act on It

- Pick a "trigger" this week that will call you to a brief prayer. This can be when you're stopped at a stop sign or a traffic light, when you start preparing or eating a meal, or when you climb stairs. Choose something that happens multiple times each day. When you encounter that trigger, call on God's name, praising Him.

- What is one specific lesson you learned this week that you want to apply daily? Write a verse or word on a card and put it in an obvious place: your bathroom mirror, your car dashboard, and so on. When you see it, ask God to help you make what you're learning in this study a daily reality.

---

1. Robert L. Hubbard Jr., *The Book of Ruth* (Grand Rapids, MI: Eerdmans, 1988), 91.
2. Sandra Richter, *The Epic of Eden* (Downers Grove, IL: IVP Academic, 2008), 158–165.

Week 1
VIDEO VIEWER GUIDE

If you ask someone, "What is your name?" you're really asking, "Tell me your

___story___."

"As for me, this is my covenant with you: You will be the father of ___many___

___nations___. No longer will you be called Abram; your name will be Abraham, for I

have made you a father of many nations. I will make you very ___fruitful___; I will

make nations of you, and kings will come from you."

Genesis 17:3-6 NIV

God also said to Abraham, "As for Sarai your wife, you are no longer to call her Sarai;

her name will be Sarah. I will bless her and will surely give you a son by her. I will bless

her so that she will be the ___mother___ of ___nations___; kings of peoples will

come from her."

Genesis 17:15-16 NIV

God sees impossibility as ___opportunity___ for ___blessing___.

What God wants to say to us is this: I have a story to tell through ___your___

___life___, and my story is ___bigger___ than the story that you've been

living.

Handwritten margin notes:

- when God wants 2 change someone, He often changes their name

- my life is suppose 2 tell his story.

- God is after changing Us not our circumstances for his glory + 4 his story.

- Our God specializes in "lost causes"

- His story stretches out over eternity, 4 ages 2 come + people will see what God has done in my life

39

Week 2
Jacob

Every Name Tells a Story: Nakusa

When I stepped off the plane in India, the sights I encountered took my breath away. The colors around me were vibrant, the smells intense, the heat, a sweltering 110 degrees. The poverty I witnessed was far beyond anything I had seen or imagined. Immense crowds of people clothed in dirt and rags, animals competing with beggars for scraps in the street, and the children—huge black eyes, unruly hair, mouths twitching at the corner as if they wished they could share a smile—they seemed to follow us everywhere we went. So many of them were begging on the streets, surrounding our mission group whenever we left the hotel and walking with us, holding out their hands. We were warned over and over not to give them anything because it would only draw more of a crowd, but my heart broke every time I saw their dirty, upturned palms.

A year later I came across an article online that brought that experience rushing back. The phrase "renaming ceremony" caught my eye in the headline, and because of my interest in names, I clicked on it and found pictures of faces just like the ones I remembered on the Indian streets.

The girls in the picture were lined up and dressed in their best, all 285 of them sharing the same name: Nakusa. This name, which is a popular one given to girls in India, means "Unwanted." In families overwhelmed by poverty, the birth of a daughter is seen as a burden, not a blessing. She's unwanted, and she hears that fact spoken aloud every time someone calls her by name. In the district where these girls live, there are only 881 girls for every 1,000 boys, a difference brought about by gender-selective abortions and neglect of baby girls to the point of death. Being unwanted is a life-threatening condition.

Concerned about the dangers facing young girls in their district, the government began furnishing free meals and education to families with girls. They even provided cash bonuses for families with girls who graduated from high school, a rare event in an area where education is usually reserved for boys. To take away the stigma of rejection, they organized a renaming ceremony for those named Nakusa and invited the girls to imagine a new future without the shame of being unwanted. These girls were reshaping their lives and choosing new futures by choosing new names. Some of the Nakusas wanted to be named after Bollywood stars, like Aishwarya. Others chose traditional names like Vaishali, which means "Prosperous, Beautiful, and Good."

One fifteen-year-old Nakusa chose to be renamed Ashmita, which means "Very Tough" or "Rock Hard" in Hindi. She commented, "Now in school, my classmates and friends will be calling me this new name, and that makes me very happy."[1] She clearly had survived events and attitudes that made her tough as nails. Now her name would reflect that.

A culture where girls are called "Unwanted" breaks my heart. But hundreds of girls who refuse to believe what they are called is a beautiful picture of hope. Just as they chose new names and new lives in one instant, we are not doomed to be named by our pasts. No matter what we have been called or how we have been treated, God longs to speak names over us that communicate His acceptance and delight in who we are. In His eyes we are treasured children, waiting to receive our new names that tell us just how wanted we truly are.

This week we will see that Jacob's life certainly started out on the wrong foot, with a name that he believed and lived out for many years. He hurt those he loved, stole what was not his, and ultimately had to flee for his life. But God had another plan, and in a renaming ceremony of His own, set Jacob on a new course in life.

Jacob's story will show us that we aren't stuck with the names and situations we start out with in life. When we enter into relationship with Jesus, we are proclaimed a "new creation"—followed by the assurance that "the old has gone, the new is here!" (2 Corinthians 5:17). God is in the business of offering us renaming ceremonies of our own. In His eyes, none of us is unwanted.

Day 1: What Name Is Given This Child?

Read God's Word

¹⁹ *This is the account of the family line of Abraham's son Isaac. Abraham became the father of Isaac,* ²⁰ *and Isaac was forty years old when he married Rebekah daughter of Bethuel the Aramean from Paddan Aram and sister of Laban the Aramean.*

²¹ *Isaac prayed to the* LORD *on behalf of his wife, because she was childless. The* LORD *answered his prayer, and his wife Rebekah became pregnant.* ²² *The babies jostled each other within her, and she said, "Why is this happening to me?" So she went to inquire of the* LORD.

²³ *The* LORD *said to her,*

"Two nations are in your womb,
and two peoples from within you will be separated;
one people will be stronger than the other,
and the older will serve the younger."

²⁴ *When the time came for her to give birth, there were twin boys in her womb.* ²⁵ *The first to come out was red, and his whole body was like a hairy garment; so they named him Esau.* ²⁶ *After this, his brother came out, with his hand grasping Esau's heel; so he was named Jacob. Isaac was sixty years old when Rebekah gave birth to them.*

Genesis 25:19-26

Reflect and Respond

I always thought it would be fun to have twins. Matching babies are so cute dressed up in identical outfits, wheeled out on display in a double stroller for the world to stop and coo over. The reality of having two babies at once is so much different than the dream world of matching outfits and adorable pictures. A close friend, blessed with twin girls, shared that there were moments when mother-hood of multiples seemed an impossible job. Her pregnancy and delivery were much more complicated and difficult. The girls arrived early and were in the NICU for weeks. And then, to her horror, they sent her and her husband home with both of them—trusting that they would know what to do! In the early days it seemed like one or both of the babies was always crying.

Rebekah and Isaac must have felt as ill prepared as any first-time parents. They had waited so long for these twin babies through the grueling journey of infertility. Rebekah's pregnancy was so difficult that she cried out to God, asking Him what was going on within her.

Reread Genesis 25:22-23. What was God's answer to Rebekah?

No mother wants there to be animosity and fighting between her children, whether it's a simple argument in the backseat or, as in this family's case, a full-blown war. In addition to a difficult pregnancy, Rebekah had the stress of knowing that her boys would cause the family constant anguish through their hostility.

After the twins were born, Rebekah and Isaac's circumstances must have been both anxious and exhausting. So I want to be as understanding as possible toward this couple of inexperienced parents when it comes to naming their twin boys. But it seems odd to me in a family with such a rich history of naming stories that they didn't put more thought into the process. In fact, they seem to have chosen the first names that popped into their heads when the boys were born. That's the only explanation I can think of for the unusual names these twins ended up with.

Reread Genesis 25:25-26. Write the names they gave their sons and the meaning of each name.

Their firstborn was covered from head to toe in red hair, so they named him Hairy, which in Hebrew was Esau. Original, right? When they got really creative with a nickname, they called the kid Edom, or Red. No baby-naming books needed here. They just went with their first impression.

As Esau was born they noticed that a little hand was tightly gripping his heel, as if to say, "Oh no you don't! I want to be first!" The new parents took one look at that little hand and named their baby Grabby, which to us is the name Jacob.

Perhaps more than in any other story in the Bible, Jacob's character was shaped from the beginning by his name. It not only reflected the circumstances of his birth, since he was grabbing at his brother's heel, but in some contexts Jacob also means "Deceiver," "Taker of What Is Not His." This unfortunate connotation had a deep impact on the person Jacob would become.

Most biblical names were given with one of two purposes: to mark the circumstances surrounding a person's birth or to describe specific character traits or gifts the child would grow to have. Jacob's name was both. His name started out as one that told the story of his birth—grabbing his brother's heel—and ended up describing the character trait for which he was best known—grabbing what was not his. The double meaning of his name had unintentional consequences as Jacob grew into his name and its character. Sometimes our names do come to have double meanings.

> Most biblical names were given with one of two purposes: to mark the circumstances surrounding a person's birth or to describe specific character traits or gifts the child would grow to have.

Read Exodus 2:1-10 to find another story of a name that grew into a double meaning.

What was the meaning of Moses' name?

In what circumstance was he discovered and given this name?

Now read Exodus 3:10. What double meaning did Moses' name have considering his calling later in life? What was he to "draw out"?

As a pastor, I find it's always an amazing privilege to baptize people, whether adults or little children. When we are baptizing children, we always begin the ceremony by asking the parents a simple question: "What name is given this child?" In answering, the parents are given a chance to state the child's name out loud to their community of faith. They are introducing the child publicly into a new family and declaring aloud the name they have chosen, the name by which this child will be known by family and friends and by God Himself.

In reality, parents answer the question "What name is given this child?" far more times than once. There is, of course, the moment they have to fill out an official birth certificate, but after that there will be countless opportunities to speak words over the child that will mark his or her future with either hope and promise or disappointment and despair. There are proper names we all go by, but there also are names that are hidden—seldom spoken descriptions that we receive branded on some internal nametag.

In some families, children are marked with beautiful, positive words that will help them grow in confidence. In others, they are scarred with words that will become unofficial nicknames of negativity, names that brand them in ways they will struggle with for a long time. If we're honest, most of our families have given us both.

I've watched a child in a tutoring program struggle over his homework, coming to a problem he could not answer and whisper to himself as he put his head down on the paper, "Stupid. Stupid. Stupid." That name came from someone, somewhere. And it stuck.

I've seen my husband fumble and drop something in the kitchen and heard the first word that popped out of his mouth: "Clumsy!"

I've struggled, too, looking in the mirror on those days when the skinny jeans just wouldn't fit (OK, let's be honest, when the not-so-skinny jeans wouldn't fit either!). There are days, too, when the task I'm trying to accomplish seems beyond my abilities or comfort zone. In those moments the adjectives that popped into my head were names of sorts, things I had been called by peers or unwitting family members who never knew their words would stick and come to the surface later in life.

What are some nicknames you've been called in life? These can be names given when you were a child (Shorty, Red, Sunshine, etc.) or names you are called because of roles or relationships (Honey, Mom, Grammy, etc.).

How do you feel when you are called those names?

What less-official nicknames—both positive and negative—are you wearing on your inner nametag?

Negative Names	**Positive Names**
(Stupid, Unworthy, Ugly, etc.)	**(Smart, Talented, etc.)**

Think of a person from your childhood or more recent past who made you feel bad about yourself. What words pop into your mind that this person might use about you?

Think of a person from your childhood or more recent past who is proud of you or gives you confidence. What words do you think this person would use to describe you? How do you feel about yourself when this person is around?

The truth is that our internal nametags are filled with both kinds of names: those that we have been given by people who shower us with encouragement and admiration, and those that have been given in careless moments of criticism. The reminder that we are also accountable for naming the people we love with our words is a sobering and sacred responsibility.

For we are God's handiwork, created in Christ Jesus to do good works, which God prepared in advance for us to do.
Ephesians 2:10

The challenge in life is to sort out the names on our internal nametags. We need to recognize and accept the names we have been given that God nods and smiles at, ones given by people speaking with God's Spirit and His character. He definitely uses people as His mouthpieces to push us forward in life to discover the identity that He has created for us.

We also need to identify which names are ones that don't fit God's vision and identity for us—harmful names spoken in haste or hate or anger, names that we will be better off allowing God to erase. For most of us, discovering and changing those names will be a lifelong endeavor, but awareness is a crucial first step.

Go back and cross out the names you wrote previously that God would not want you to continue to wear on your inner nametag.

The names that matter, the names that should stick, are the names given us by our heavenly Father. The Bible is full of the beautiful, life-giving names that God so lovingly gives us. Here is just a sample.

Read each of the following passages and list the powerful and positive names given to us by God.

Judges 6:12

Isaiah 41:9-10

Ephesians 2:10

1 Corinthians 3:16-17

1 Peter 2:9

God often speaks to us through His words in Scripture. He can also speak through people who love and affirm us. And on certain occasions He speaks directly to our hearts. The names God gives are the ones that should stick for a lifetime. All others must fade away to make room for His dreams for us.

If God could replace the negative nicknames on your heart with positive ones, reflecting His feelings and goals for you, what would your new names be? List them below. (Examples: Forgiven, Healed, Child of God, Confident, Beautiful)

Jacob's story teaches us that words matter, no matter how small. As we continue to follow his story throughout the week, I hope it also will teach us that no name is permanent if God wants to change it. It doesn't matter how it is given or who gives it or how much it seems to mark us for life; God always has the power to start us over on a better-named path, showering us with His grace.

Pray About It

Ask God to continue making you aware of the names that need to be removed from your internal nametag. As you go about your day, be aware of the words you speak in your internal monologue. When you are using words or names for yourself that are not positive, stop and ask God to help you replace those with His vision and names for you.

Act on It

- Think about the people in your life you've been given influence over. These can be family members, coworkers, or friends. How can God use you to "name" them this week?

Day 2: Brotherly Love

Read God's Word

[27] *The boys grew up, and Esau became a skillful hunter, a man of the open country, while Jacob was content to stay at home among the tents.* [28] *Isaac, who had a taste for wild game, loved Esau, but Rebekah loved Jacob.*
[29] *Once when Jacob was cooking some stew, Esau came in from the open country, famished.* [30] *He said to Jacob, "Quick, let me have some of that red stew! I'm famished!" (That is why he was also called Edom.)*
[31] *Jacob replied, "First sell me your birthright."*
[32] *"Look, I am about to die," Esau said. "What good is the birthright to me?"*
[33] *But Jacob said, "Swear to me first." So he swore an oath to him, selling his birthright to Jacob.*

God always has the power to start us over on a better-named path, showering us with His grace.

34 Then Jacob gave Esau some bread and some lentil stew. He ate and drank, and then got up and left.

So Esau despised his birthright.

Genesis 25:27-34

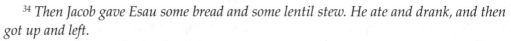

Reflect and Respond

I grew up longing for a sister who would be a friend and playmate. In my daydreams, she and I would share clothes, do each other's hair, and tell secrets that made us laugh. While I was great at sisterly love in my daydream world, I wasn't very good at it in the closest sister relationship I had in real life. During my elementary school years, we lived one block away from my stepfather's sister and her family. I had two step-cousins who were very close to me in age. Chelsey, the oldest of the two, was only a year behind me in school. We grew up playing together daily, sleeping over at each other's houses, going to the same school, and getting involved in the same activities. That last part was where things started to get tough. I was excited to start taking dance lessons. Chelsey signed up for the same class and pirouetted beside me at the recital. I joined the children's choir at church. Chelsey and I competed for the same solos. I signed up for the tennis team. Guess who was there, across the net, hitting balls back in my face?

Although we didn't live in the same house, my feelings for Chelsey were a lot like those my friends described having toward their siblings. One minute I loved having a friend and a playmate who was around all the time; another minute I was overwhelmed with feelings of jealousy and competition. I didn't like sharing the family spotlight. I treated her one minute like the sister I longed for and the next like a distrusted adversary. As we got older and the issues of competition had higher stakes, I pushed our friendship further and further away. Looking back, I wish I'd embraced what could have been a lifelong closeness instead of holding her at arm's length.

Siblings, cousins, and other close family members are often our first play-mates, our first friends, and our first enemies—our first reality check that the world does not revolve around us. They help us define who we are and how we will treat others for a lifetime.

This certainly was true for Jacob and Esau. Their sibling rivalry began early: in the womb. As we read yesterday, their mother even cried out to God because their prenatal scuffles were so painful. As soon as they were born, their inheri-tance and place in the family was sealed for life.

When his twin brother, Esau, beat him to the finish line to be born first by a matter of minutes, Jacob's position for life was supposedly decided. As the second-born, Jacob would have inherited only a fraction of his parents' wealth, while Esau would receive a larger share called the birthright. Then, upon their father's death, Esau would receive the blessing as well, a spiritual inheritance on top of the final confirmation of the material one. This meant the elder would succeed the father as patriarch of the family and the younger would be subservient to his sibling as the ruler and owner of the estate as well as the spiritual leader. Being first definitely had its perks!

This hierarchy certainly played a part in the conflict between the two brothers. There also were other factors that contributed to the discord.

Reread Genesis 25:27-28. What do we learn in these verses about the relationship Jacob and Esau had with each of their parents?

Jacob wasn't going to settle for second. His name, innocently given as a reminder of his hand on his brother's chubby heel, could also mean "Deceiver, Supplanter, Swindler"—one who grabs hold of what is not his own and takes it. And grab Jacob did.

One day when he saw the moment to take advantage of his brother, he grabbed it. His older brother, Esau, was a hairy, ruddy, outdoorsy type. He came home famished from a long hunting trip to find that his irritating little brother, Jacob, had just dished himself up the last bowl of food in the house. Today we'd just grab some microwavable meal and the whole issue would be over in sixty seconds, but this was a day when the recipe for chicken nuggets started with the instructions "Go in the backyard and kill a chicken." Preparing a meal could take all day, and Esau was hungry *now*.

Jacob milked the situation for all it was worth. He was younger, and younger children know that, generally, they can't win in strength, so they have to win in strategy. You have to devise a plan that is going to get you either beaten up or a really good trade.

Reread Genesis 25:29-34 and answer the following questions.

What did Esau ask of Jacob?

What did Jacob ask for in return, and how did he guarantee it?

How did Jacob take advantage of Esau in this situation?

How did Esau respond?

birthright—material inheritance and authority given only to firstborn

blessing—spiritual blessing and confirmation of inheritance given just before father's death

49

Be devoted to one another in love. Honor one another above yourselves.
Romans 12:10

Why settle for one bowl of food when someday you will own all the bowls in the house, not to mention the house itself? I'd like to look down my nose at Esau for his shortsightedness, but the truth is that instant gratification sometimes gets the best of all of us. At one time or another, we've all looked at something right in front of us that, if chosen, would mean serious long-term consequences, and cried out, "Go for it!" Short-term pleasure is gratifying, but long-term regrets can be shattering. We know they were for Esau.

Have some stew. Lose your birthright. By no means a fair deal.

Jacob, too, experienced a gain and a loss in that moment. He gained exactly what he set out to grab in the first place. But what he lost was of great value as well. First, he lost a brother. They shared a womb, and parents, and a home, and now there was a rift there that would take an act of God to repair. He also lost any sense of goodness in himself as he surrendered to the dark side of his name. He spent the first half of his story struggling to take what was not rightfully his. We'll see him complete the plan and then spend the second half of his life running away from the mistakes he made.

Jacob's epic struggle with the motivations within himself pulled him in two very different directions. His struggle raises an important question we must ask ourselves: *Do I grab onto things for my own gain while leaving my relationships in the dust?* There's a saying I love about the best rule to use when determining priorities: "People are more important than things." It seems simple, but that lesson is hard to learn when you're a small child whose brother or sister has a toy that you want. It's just as hard to learn when you're a grownup, hungry to fill some urge that will inevitably diminish a relationship that matters to you. What we fail to see when we grab what we want in the short-term is that the relationships we overlook are worth far more in the long-term.

Learning to put relationships with others before personal gain is definitely not something that comes naturally. God urges us to break the easy pattern of putting ourselves first.

Read Philippians 2:3-4 and Romans 12:10 and answer the following questions:

How would these verses have changed Jacob's life, his family, and his relationship with his brother if he had applied this wisdom?

How would they change yours?

Is there someone whose life and actions seem to embody these verses? Write her or his name or initials below and describe what you've seen in this individual.

As we learn to treat others with respect and honor, it's important that we not disrespect ourselves in the process. The commandment to "Love your neighbor as yourself" comes with the implication that we *first* must be able to love ourselves without reservation. If we cannot, the step of loving our neighbor will always be tainted with neediness and self-interest. But if we love and serve others in an overflow of self-respect and acceptance, we will offer ourselves out of an understanding of God's love for us. Once we understand our own worth in Christ, it is easy to want others to feel special and valued in the same way.

Take a look at some of the specific guidelines given in Scripture for how we are to treat one another. Look up each passage and summarize it in a few words.

Romans 15:7

1 Corinthians 1:10

Ephesians 4:2

1 Thessalonians 5:11

Galatians 6:2

Luke 6:31

Ironically, I sometimes find these commands more difficult to keep toward the people who are closest to me—even family members. For some reason, their flaws and failings are harder for me to overlook than those of acquaintances.

As twins, Jacob and Esau had the closest possible of human connections. They also had the greatest temptation toward competition and contempt. The closer we are to the people in our lives, the more our familiarity can tempt us to treat them with disrespect. At the same time, our closeness can help us discover the amazing gifts God places in each individual. The relationships that are part of your everyday life have the potential to make you a jealous Jacob, or you can choose to celebrate the gift of your close relationships and the handiwork of God you find there. Ask God to help you to see the masterpieces He has created in others and praise Him for the hidden gifts they bring to your life.

Pray About It

Think of one person you have difficulty loving and serving. Ask God in prayer to help you . . .

- consider this person better than yourself (Philippians 2:3)
- accept the person (Romans 15:7)
- be patient with this person (Ephesians 4:2)
- carry his or her burdens, especially in prayer (Galatians 6:2)

Reach out in humility to this person today.

Act on It

- Do you know a family or families that you admire for their close, loving relationships and acceptance of one another? Seek them out and tell them that you think highly of their family. Ask them their secret of closeness and acceptance.

- Do you have a sibling or someone you grew up with that you competed with in some way? How is that relationship today? Think of one small step you can take today to improve that relationship, and then act on it.

Day 3: More Than Enough

Read God's Word

[1] *When Isaac was old and his eyes were so weak that he could no longer see, he called for Esau his older son and said to him, "My son."*

"Here I am," he answered.

[2] *Isaac said, "I am now an old man and don't know the day of my death.* [3] *Now then, get your weapons—your quiver and bow—and go out to the open country to hunt some wild game for me.* [4] *Prepare me the kind of tasty food I like and bring it to me to eat, so that I may give you my blessing before I die."*

[5] *Now Rebekah was listening as Isaac spoke to his son Esau. When Esau left for the open country to hunt game and bring it back,* [6] *Rebekah said to her son Jacob, "Look, I overheard your father say to your brother Esau,* [7] *'Bring me some game and prepare me*

some tasty food to eat, so that I may give you my blessing in the presence of the LORD before I die.' ⁸ Now, my son, listen carefully and do what I tell you: ⁹ Go out to the flock and bring me two choice young goats, so I can prepare some tasty food for your father, just the way he likes it. ¹⁰ Then take it to your father to eat, so that he may give you his blessing before he dies."

¹¹ Jacob said to Rebekah his mother, "But my brother Esau is a hairy man, and I'm a man with smooth skin. ¹² What if my father touches me? I would appear to be tricking him and would bring down a curse on myself rather than a blessing."

¹³ His mother said to him, "My son, let the curse fall on me. Just do what I say; go and get them for me."

Genesis 27:1-13

Reflect and Respond

I'll be happy when . . .

I must have finished this sentence a hundred times in my life. I'll be happy when I get my degree. When I have a job. When I find my soul mate. When he proposes. When we can afford a bigger house. When we finally have the children we long for.

This last one was a biggie for me. Our years of struggle with infertility and miscarriage were a constant rollercoaster of hope and disappointment. Grief is usually an emotion we feel for someone who is no longer with us. But my husband and I struggled with grief for someone who had not yet arrived. Grief for the children we longed for. Grief for the ones we lost. Grief for our dreams. The pain of those moments made me wish for another life, another reality. It made me think happiness was something always just over the horizon, never within reach.

There were bright spots, such as relationships that deepened because I needed someone to lean on. I realized that there were a handful of friends I could call on at any time. My husband and I turned to each other for comfort and found we had a depth in our marriage we didn't know existed. I would love to tell you that I turned to God consistently, like I thought a good Christian should, and that I found spiritual comfort there from my pain. The truth is that sometimes I didn't feel like talking to God at all. Sometimes I felt like He wasn't in the room when I cried out to Him, or I felt angry that He wasn't answering my prayers. When I looked around and saw friends with their children, I wondered why He loved others enough to give them their hearts' desire when mine went unfulfilled.

53

What is an area of your life in which you struggle to be content?

Complete the following sentence:

I'll be happy when _____.

> "I have loved you with an everlasting love; I have drawn you with unfailing kindness."
> Jeremiah 31:3

I'll be happy when. . . . Jacob seems to have lived by that motto. He grew up staring across the table at his brother, who was to receive the birthright and blessing, and dreaming of a day he could have them for himself. Riddled with envy and discontent, Jacob spent his childhood and early adulthood longing for what was not his and scheming how to get it. His attitude toward his brother and his parents was shadowed in a cloud of discontent and dishonesty.

Is there a person or group of people that you've had an attitude of envy toward? If so, how has it affected your relationship with them?

Jacob made the mistake of determining his happiness based on what his brother had. Our worth isn't determined by how we measure up against other people; it is determined by how God loves us.

What does each of these Scriptures help you understand about God's love for us and the relationship between that love and our love for others?

Psalm 45:11

Jeremiah 31:3

1 John 4:9-12

1 John 4:19-21

Truthfully, Jacob had help developing this attitude. As with most family problems, the issues between Jacob and his brother, Esau, didn't just spring up out of nowhere. They had been brewing in the genes and behavior of this unusual family for generations. As we learned yesterday, the ways that Isaac and Rebekah treated their boys contributed to the conflict between the brothers.

Read again Genesis 25:28 and fill in the blanks below:

"Isaac . . . loved _____, but Rebekah loved _____." (NIV)

How do you think this favoritism might have fostered a sense of competition and unhappiness?

Though Esau and Jacob must have felt special at times because of the preferential treatment they received, the favoritism shown to one of them no doubt was hurtful to the other. Whatever someone's reason for showing preferential treatment, it often communicates to us that we are not good enough, that we haven't earned the right to his or her love.

Have you ever experienced or witnessed the dynamic of favoritism—in family relationships or other close relationships? If so, how did it affect you and/or others?

As today's reading from God's Word reveals, Jacob's chance to finally possess both the birthright and the blessing came when his father, Isaac, lay dying. Isaac knew he wanted to pass the blessing along to his older son, so he sent Esau out to hunt for and prepare a last meal. That's when Rebekah moved into manipulation mode, engaging Jacob in her plan of deceit that would ultimately divide their family.

Reread Genesis 27:9. What did Rebekah ask Jacob to do?

Now read Genesis 27:14-17. What else did Rebekah's plan of deceit involve?

Rebekah's plot involved preparing a meal, dressing Jacob in his brother's clothes that she happened to have ready for such an occasion, and putting goatskins on Jacob's hands and neck to cover his smooth skin. The story suggests this was a premeditated act she had been planning for some time as she schemed about how to steal from her older son to favor the younger.

Read Genesis 27:18-29 to see how Rebekah's plan of deceit unfolded.

Clearly Isaac was unsure that this was really his son Esau. What questions and "tests" did he use to settle his uncertainty (vv. 20-22)? What finally convinced him (v. 23)?

What hopes for his son did Isaac convey in his blessing (vv. 28-29)?

God never operates according to the principle of scarcity. He is never limited in how many prayers He can answer or how much love He can pour out.

Favoritism is the notion that in order to give a fuller measure of love to one person, we must neglect or deprive another. Judging from their actions, both Rebekah and Isaac believed this to be true, and they could not have been more wrong.

Of all the commodities that families provide one another—shelter, food, quality time, love—love is the one resource that isn't ever limited or scarce. When we share love, affection, and approval with another person, our storehouse is not depleted but multiplied.

Families are sometimes programmed to act with a sense of scarcity, as if we have to choose who receives love and praise and blessing because they are in short supply. Our lack of contentment is often rooted in the feeling that we weren't given enough by our families of origin—enough love, praise, or attention.

The heart-wrenching final scene in this story is a picture of a son begging for approval and blessing, while a father believes there's no more to offer because he has already given it all away to the wrong son. Scarcity is the controlling idea on his side of the parenting equation, as well as his wife's.

Read Genesis 27:30-40. How would you describe the emotions expressed in this scene?

How does Esau's blessing compare to Jacob's (vv. 39-40)?

The good news is that God never operates according to the principle of scarcity. He is never limited in how many prayers He can answer or how much love He can pour out. Just because God loves and blesses one of His children doesn't mean He can't love and bless all the others. In fact, He knows specifically how to offer each of us answers to our unique needs. When we keep our eyes on the blessings other people seem to have, we lose the point of the contentment that comes from knowing our heavenly Father provides all our needs.

What do these verses say about the abundance and generosity of our heavenly Father?

Psalm 50:9-12

Matthew 7:9-11

Ephesians 4:32

When we, God's children, are behaving at our best, He showers us with love and blessings. And when we are at our worst, He still showers us with love and blessings. The idea that God favors one child over another is simply untrue. God's acts of abundance are in direct contrast with the world's belief in supply and demand. Unlike Jacob and Esau's parents, God is a Divine Parent who is able to give with equal abundance, working for the best for each of His children, even when it's not apparent to us in the present.

My own struggle with contentment didn't end when our son was born. I'll admit that even in the midst of joy and praise and thankfulness, I still had my moments of discontent. "I'll be happy when I have the child I long for" quickly gave way to the cry of "I'll be happy if he'll just sleep through the night!" Answered prayers are often quickly followed by new prayer requests—proof that contentment doesn't lie in having our every whim fulfilled.

Contentment is not a product of having everything our hearts desire. It's a commodity produced by internal, not external, circumstances. Waiting for our situation to change before we'll be happy means we will always find another longing around the next corner.

Read Philippians 4:11-13. Rewrite the message of these verses by completing the sentence below to reflect your own situation.

I have learned to be content no matter what—no matter if I have _____ or don't have _____ .

All of us have areas in our lives where we struggle to be content. If we're not careful, our discontent will damage our relationships with the people around us. Discontent also damages our relationship with God. A life spent wishing you had what someone else has shortchanges the life God intended you to live. When we become so focused on the blessings in other people's lives, like Jacob did, we

57

ignore our own and miss a chance to praise God for the blessings He has given us. We are basically saying to God, "I don't appreciate what You've given me or how You've created me. I'd rather switch lives with someone else."

Read 1 Timothy 6:6-10.

What are the results of being content?

What are the results of being discontent?

> Contentment . . . takes work and trust, and it is nurtured by worship, praise, and gratitude.

Contentment doesn't come on like a light bulb when we flip a switch. It takes work and trust, and it is nurtured by worship, praise, and gratitude. These acts change our perspective. They help us focus on God's blessings in our own lives instead of looking over the fence at someone else's blessings; they help us treasure our own birthright and blessing instead of trading them away because we long for what is just out of reach.

Knowing the love of our heavenly Father means knowing there will always be more than enough to go around.

Pray About It

Take time in prayer for confession, acceptance, and petition.

Confession: Confess the ways in which you have been discontent with your life. When have you felt that God favors others over you? When has your happiness been focused on wanting what others have rather than seeing what God has given you?

Acceptance: Pray over the ways that God has blessed you. Accept that you are His favored child, that He loves you unconditionally, that there is no one in the world that He loves more than you.

Petition: Ask God to help you see and accept His blessings in your life today. Ask for His protection against the temptations of envy and discontentment.

Act on It

- Find a time when you can focus on worship, praise, and gratitude this week. Listen to praise music that turns your heart toward God in worship.

- Keep a gratitude journal that reminds you to praise God for your blessings.

- Look for someone who has far less than you and serve him or her this week.

Day 4: The Divine Wrestling Match

Read God's Word

22 That night Jacob got up and took his two wives, his two maidservants and his eleven sons and crossed the ford of the Jabbok. 23 After he had sent them across the stream, he sent over all his possessions. 24 So Jacob was left alone, and a man wrestled with him till daybreak. 25 When the man saw that he could not overpower him, he touched the socket of Jacob's hip so that his hip was wrenched as he wrestled with the man. 26 Then the man said, "Let me go, for it is daybreak."

But Jacob replied, "I will not let you go unless you bless me."

27 The man asked him, "What is your name?"

"Jacob," he answered.

28 Then the man said, "Your name will no longer be Jacob, but Israel, because you have struggled with God and with men and have overcome."

29 Jacob said, "Please tell me your name."

But he replied, "Why do you ask my name?" Then he blessed him there.

30 So Jacob called the place Peniel, saying, "It is because I saw God face to face, and yet my life was spared."

Genesis 32:22-30

Reflect and Respond

Tim sat across the table from me, his head in his hands, telling me his story. It wasn't an easy one to tell. His struggle with addiction and control had left permanent scars on those he loved most. One of his daughters had entered young adulthood with all the baggage from growing up with a dad who put his addiction before his family. Now she was struggling in her own fight with a devastating drug habit, which had come close to destroying the life of her young daughter.

Tim and his wife were taking steps to turn their family around. They had begun attending church, sought counseling, and obtained guardianship of their young granddaughter. Watching this little girl that he loved so much grow up before his eyes made Tim long for true change. He was desperate to do things differently this time around, to have a positive impact on this generation after he had messed up so badly with the one before.

As his family tried to plug into our community for support, he told me that he was trying to reach out and form friendships but that he often felt like a misfit. Everyone around him seemed to have it together. He wasn't sure how to be real about his own problems in a church and neighborhood where every time he asked how they were, people smiled and said they were "fine." Tim didn't feel fine. How could he find a way to belong here?

Tim's counselor encouraged him to get involved in a community of others who were struggling to overcome addiction. When he walked into his first meeting, he was shocked to see so many of his perfect-looking neighbors. It was a room full of people who looked like they had it all together but were falling apart on the inside.

Tim told me about one woman who never would have struck him as someone with any problems at all. She was perfectly put together, wearing an immaculate and expensive outfit. She told the group that as she gained control over her addiction to alcohol, she had replaced that addiction with a compulsive spending habit. Her spiral into debt was so out of control that it looked like her family might lose their home.

"Our mortgage hasn't been paid in full in months," she said as she straightened out her designer outfit. "But you'd better believe our country club dues are up to date. We wouldn't want to look bad to our neighbors!"

That's when Tim had an "aha!" moment. He said, "I realized I had been comparing my insides to everyone else's outsides." He knew all too well the mess of what he was wrestling with, but he never spent much time thinking about the fact that everyone he met was struggling in some way.

When have you compared your insides to someone else's outsides? How did it make you feel?

Do you find it hard to believe that everyone you meet is struggling in some way? Why or why not?

Judging from the outside, Jacob was a success. He had a large family, livestock, and wealth. But on the inside, he was an absolute mess! In fact, most of his story was a tragedy of his own making. He spent his life grabbing at what was not his, poisoning the relationships that should have sustained him. Instead of being able to enjoy what he worked so immorally to gain, he ran from his mistakes, wrestling with an identity and a past that were toxic to him and to those he loved.

Despite his material success, Jacob was dissatisfied. Whether it was maturity, nostalgia, or regret, he began to miss what he had left behind enough to face the consequences of his actions and return to the scene of his crimes. He finally mustered the courage to gather up his entourage (which looked more like a traveling circus than a family road trip) and make the long trek back to his homeland.

On the very last leg of his journey, Jacob learned that he was about to encounter the one person he needed to make amends with, his brother, Esau. The night before the confrontation, Jacob took everything he had accumulated—everything and everyone he had grabbed, deceived, or swindled to get—and sent them across a river called Jabbok, which means "Emptying." Then he sat down alone.

Finally, Jacob was by himself in the quiet to consider all that he had done with his life. It probably was the first time Jacob had been alone with his thoughts in a long time—only he wasn't alone for long.

Reread Genesis 32:24 and fill in the blank:

"So Jacob was left alone, and a _____ wrestled with him till daybreak."
(NIV)

Biblical scholars are divided on exactly who this "man" was that wrestled with Jacob in Genesis 32. Was it God, a man, or God's representative in angelic form?

Reread Genesis 32:25-26, 30. Then read Hosea 12:3-4. Why do you think opinions differ about who wrestled with Jacob?

Several other places in the Bible use the word "man" to describe what some scholars interpret as a visitation from the Divine.

Read Genesis 18:1-15 and Daniel 3:24-25. Would you recognize these incidences as visitations from God?

This all-night wrestling match was clearly a Divine encounter. Not only does the reference in Hosea 12 let us know that God was present here; the authority we see the mysterious wrestling partner display in renaming Jacob is the same authority displayed by God in renaming Jacob's grandparents. Those clues help us see that God showed up in person in Jacob's hour of need. That night forced Jacob to stop grasping at things and ambitions and grab hold of God Himself. Still, Jacob was bold enough to ask his wrestling partner for a blessing.

Reread Genesis 32:27. When Jacob asked for a blessing, what did his wrestling partner ask him, and what was Jacob's answer?

The last time Jacob had asked for a blessing (from his father), he had lied, misrepresented himself, and taken on the identity of his brother. This time when Jacob asked for a blessing (from his heavenly Father), he was again asked in return, "What is your name?" His answer was both an introduction and a confession: "I am Jacob," he said truthfully. Deceiver. Swindler. Taker of what is not mine.

God must have been satisfied with that answer, because He knew it took a lot for Jacob to speak the truth at last. Even so, He wasn't satisfied with the man standing before Him. God wants to hear our honest confession and assessment of who we are and where we find ourselves, but that doesn't mean He'll leave us that way. Only when we are honest about our desperate state and our desperate need for Him can He set about changing us to become the ones He wants us to be.

Reread Genesis 32:28. What new name did God give to Jacob, and why?

At that moment, Jacob the Deceiver no longer existed. The man left limping at daybreak was now Israel—which means "He Who Wrestles with God." The nation that once was promised to Abraham and Sarah now had a name. They were the children of Israel—the ones who wrestle with God.

But that isn't the end of the story. Jacob went on to ask the name of his wrestling partner. We will explore this in greater depth tomorrow. For now, take note of the answer Jacob's wrestling partner gave and how Jacob responded.

Reread Genesis 32:29-30.

What answer did Jacob's wrestling partner give (v. 29)?

What did Jacob name the place, and why (v. 30)?

Write the meaning of each name in this story in the chart below to remind yourself of its significance:

Name	Meaning	New Name	Meaning
Jacob		Israel	
Jabbok			
Peniel			

> Change is inevitable when we encounter God.

Change is inevitable when we encounter God. Like Jacob, my friend Tim began to find healing because he was honest with God—and with others—about who he was; he confessed that his life had become a mess of his own making. When he stopped trying to manage the mess himself and turned it over to God, He found God was giving him a chance at a new identity.

When have you clung to something besides God?

What forced or encouraged you to let go?

Jacob learned that the more he grasped at things, the more he lost. The more he let go, the more he gained.

Read what Matthew 16:24-26 says about this irony of gaining something by letting go. Paraphrase this passage in your own words below:

> The fact that God loves us and chooses us is no guarantee that we won't struggle. But it is a guarantee that we won't struggle alone.

If we cling to anything but God, even if we cling to our own self-sufficiency or our own false identities, we will find ourselves sinking into a pit we've dug for ourselves. But if we let go and grab hold of God, we'll discover that we're closer to finding the peace, forgiveness, and transformation we long for. Those who pretend otherwise are still clinging to a lie.

The fact that God loves us and chooses us is no guarantee that we won't struggle. But it is a guarantee that we won't struggle alone.

Instead of leaving Jacob alone in his time of struggle, God wrestled with Him through one of the most difficult times in his life. He also renamed him Israel, indicating that God would continue to wrestle with him—and with the people who would follow in his family—when times were tough.

Read Isaiah 43:1-7. What does God promise in this passage about the difficult times in our lives?

Looking back at the tough times in your life, has there been a time when you knew without a doubt that God was with you? If so, describe how you knew at the time, or how you know, in retrospect, that God joined you in your struggle.

When we wrestle with the issues of life—even issues we've brought on ourselves, like Jacob—God will be right there wrestling with us, bringing us an outcome of blessing, even when we don't deserve it. God will always be there to offer a new blessing, a new name, and a new chance to be declared His children.

Pray about It

On a piece of paper, draw your own river Jabbok ("Emptying"). On one side, list the things you've been clinging to for security, safety, and significance.

On the other side, write your name and God's name. On this side, write a prayer asking God to help you cling only to Him and nothing else for security.

Act on It

- Think of someone you know who is struggling through a difficult time. Maybe she or he is struggling with illness or caring for someone who is ill or aging. Maybe there are difficulties in this person's family, job, or school. List below three practical ways you can help this person know she or he is not alone in the struggle. Pick one to act on this week.

Day 5: Revelation: The Unspeakable Name

Read God's Word

²⁹ *Jacob said, "Please tell me your name."*
But he replied, "Why do you ask my name?" Then he blessed him there.
³⁰ *So Jacob called the place Peniel, saying, "It is because I saw God face to face, and yet my life was spared."*

Genesis 32:29-30

¹³ *Moses said to God, "Suppose I go to the Israelites and say to them, 'The God of your fathers has sent me to you,' and they ask me, 'What is his name?' Then what shall I tell them?"*
¹⁴ *God said to Moses, "I AM WHO I AM. This is what you are to say to the Israelites: 'I AM has sent me to you.'"*
¹⁵ *God also said to Moses, "Say to the Israelites, 'The LORD, the God of your fathers—the God of Abraham, the God of Isaac and the God of Jacob—has sent me to you. 'This is my name forever, the name you shall call me from generation to generation."*

Exodus 3:13-15

Reflect and Respond

The most important part of any phone call is the first three seconds.

When I answer my phone with a chipper "hello," the response on the other end of the line determines the level and depth of the rest of the conversation. The person on the other end of the line hardly ever gives his or her own name (unless it's our first conversation). Usually, though, the way the person says *my* name tells me exactly who it is.

> "Hello . . . "
> "Hey, Jes!"
> "Hi, sweetie."
> "Reverend LaGrone, do you have a minute to talk?"
> "Mommy, guess what!"

The name others use when addressing me is a gift I've offered them, something I have given them unspoken permission to use. It often reveals the depth of our relationship or the role I play in their lives, and they in mine. It also reveals the type of authority or influence they have over me. Whether we realize it or not, the name we give someone to call us and the way in which the person says it is a defining part of our connection—relational currency to be spent wisely.

What name does God give us to address Him? The answer tells us so much about how He wants our relationship to play out. Are we supposed to hold Him at arm's length, put Him on an unreachable pedestal, or treat Him like a casual acquaintance?

As we saw yesterday, the night that Jacob wrestled with God, he demanded to know his opponent's name. But if we look beyond the surface, we discover that this wasn't a request for a formal introduction: "Hey there, I'm Jacob. And you are . . . ?" Actually, it was a not-so-subtle move toward checkmate, an attempt at domination. Asking his opponent's name was the same as asking his wrestling partner to cry "uncle!" Since a name contained someone's essence, the heart of his or her story, knowing someone's true name meant having a measure of authority and control over him or her. To be able to call someone by name meant having a sense of familiarity and power. Jacob wanted his opponent's name because he wanted to win.

Even in this Divine encounter in Genesis 32, when Jacob was given one more chance at redemption and rebirth, he had the audacity to try to grab one more thing for himself: the name of God.

If you flip forward to the next book of the Bible, Exodus, you'll find Moses also in the middle of a desperate encounter with God. At the burning bush God called Moses to lead God's people out of slavery in Egypt and into a beautiful and plentiful Promised Land. When God gave him his marching orders, Moses knew better than to go back and stand in front of the crowd of Israelites without some credentials. He knew they would ask "Who sent you? Who commanded you to do this?" Moses needed some clout. He needed to be able to communicate to the people that the One who was spinning this audacious plan would have the power to carry it out, that the One who was calling them would also lead them. Moses actually needed to be reassured of this more than anyone! If God's people (and their leader) ever needed to know they could trust Him, this was the time. And before they could know they could *trust* Him, they had to *know* Him.

Read Exodus 3. Why does Moses want to know God's name?

God responded by giving a name to His people that would both reveal more about Him and make Him more of a mystery.

Reread Exodus 3:14. How did God answer Moses?

God said to Moses, "___ _____ WHO ___ _____. This is what you are to say to the Israelites: '___ _____ has sent me to you.' " (NIV)

In Hebrew the name "I AM" is made up of four consonants: YHWH. This ancient name for God is known as the *tetragrammaton*, and it is derived from a verb meaning "to be."

Reflect on a God whose name is "I AM." What might that mean?

A word made up entirely of consonants is unpronounceable. Try saying jxtpstn or schtlgy out loud! God's people needed a way to address Him, a way to speak the unspeakable YHWH. But they were afraid. They didn't want to mistakenly pull a "Jacob," trying to make a power play toward God by grabbing hold of His name. They were afraid of addressing God with too much familiarity.

Because of the understanding that to speak the name of someone aloud was to try to exert a measure of power or control over him or her, they regarded God's name, YHWH, as too sacred to pronounce. They took the instruction of Leviticus 24:16, "Anyone who blasphemes the name of YHWH must be put to death," so seriously that they went a step further by implying that anyone who even *pronounced* the name of YHWH aloud would be in deep trouble. God never said that was the case, but they figured that when dealing with the Holy One, it was better to be safe than sorry.

To avoid pronouncing God's name aloud, God's people deliberately took the consonants God gave Moses and added the vowels from another word. So, they took the name YHWH, I AM, and added the vowels from another title for God, Adonai, which means "My Lord." Mixed together, these are pronounced *Yahweh* or *Jehovah*. So, when God's name is spelled out in the Old Testament as Yahweh or Jehovah, it's actually a divine mashup of two different titles—a holy

> When God's name is spelled out in the Old Testament as Yahweh or Jehovah, it's actually a divine mashup of two different titles—a holy hodge-podge of letters intended to make sure no one took liberties with the name of the Almighty.

hodgepodge of letters intended to make sure no one took liberties with the name of the Almighty.

Even today, many Jews still refer to Jehovah simply as *Hashem*, which means, "The Name." Some Jewish references to God remove the vowel and spell the word G*D or G_D so that no one will accidentally pronounce it out loud.

I sometimes wonder if we've lost our sense of awe at God's holiness—His nature that is bigger, greater, better than anything else we know in this life. In order to help people understand the personal nature of God, we try so hard to communicate God's accessibility, approachability, closeness, and friendly nature that we portray Him as our buddy, our copilot, our divine BFF.

When I pray, I like to picture Jesus walking next to me or sitting across a table from me. His humanity makes me feel comfortable and at ease. But I forget sometimes to honor His divinity as well, His holiness. Imagine having such reverence and awe for the powerful holiness of God that you dare not even speak His name out loud. Those who sought to protect the name of YHWH from anyone who would misuse it had great respect for the holiness of God's name.

Look up these verses about the transcendence of God—the trait of God's personality that we understand as holy, other, set apart. Write a couple of words describing God for each.

Exodus 15:11

Isaiah 6:1-3

Revelation 1:12-19

Look up these verses about the immanence of God—the trait of God's personality that we understand as approachable, close, accessible. Write a couple of words describing God for each.

Genesis 3:8

John 1:14

Read Isaiah 57:15. This verse describes both God's immanence (close) and transcendence (apart). Can you identify which part of the verse describes which characteristic?

When you pray to God, are you more likely to imagine Him as immanent or transcendent? Why?

When Jacob asked God His name, God refused to give it to him. When Moses asked, God simply answered: "I AM."

For both of these men, God revealed more about Himself through His actions than through any name spoken aloud. Instead of offering them a name they could call to have power over Him, God revealed His nature to them by intervening with power in the events of their lives.

I love the fact that God isn't aloof or deliberately mysterious. He is constantly revealing, through His actions in our lives and our world, who He is and what He is capable of.

In Week 1 we saw the self-revealing nature of God in the lives of Abraham and Sarah. Although they never asked for God's name, God proclaimed to them: *I will. I will. I will.* (See Week 1: Day 2.) God made a promise and followed through with actions. Not only is God a God of being (I AM); our God is a God of action, of doing (I will).

> I AM is a statement of who God is.
> I will is a statement of what God does.

God reveals Himself to us by declaring who He is through the words of Scripture, but He doesn't stop there. He also names Himself by putting those words into action, revealing His power, love, and forgiveness in our lives. This high and lofty God, who is so powerful that many dared not even speak His name out loud, is constantly naming Himself by giving visible proof of His attributes. What's better, a God who tells you that He's powerful, loving, patient, and good, or a God who shows you these traits in every interaction He has with His people? If given the same choice in my relationships with people, I'd choose actions over words every time. Better to have a friend who silently acts on her or his good will than who professes good and then acts differently when your back is turned. Thankfully, we serve and love a God who will never separate words and actions.

One of the awesome things about God is that His "I will" and His "I AM" are never out of step with each other. When someone's actions are consistent and reflective of his or her character, he or she has integrity. God exists in a state of integrity, literally the integration of who He is and what He does. In other words, God always acts in ways defined by who He is at His core.

> [God] is constantly revealing, through His actions in our lives and our world, who He is and what He is

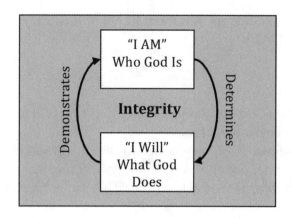

The integrity of God means that who He is *determines* what He does. His actions flow out of the goodness, power, and holiness of His name. Likewise, what God does *demonstrates* who He is. The character of God shows us that we can trust Him. He will never act in ways that are not established in Scripture. God's actions are consistent with His character.

Read the following Scriptures. What does each reveal about God's unchanging nature?

Lamentations 3:22-23

Psalm 55:22

John 10:28

Hebrews 13:8

What does this tell us about our ability to trust God?

Perhaps God's reluctance to articulate His name to scoundrels like Jacob and leaders like Moses had little to do with their ability to control Him by speaking it aloud. Maybe it had more to do with the fact that the nature of God is best discovered not through some word on the tip of our tongues but through following Him, observing His actions, and discovering His nature through His fingerprints in the world.

Soon after God's life-changing and name-changing meeting with Jacob, He began to identify Himself as "The God of Abraham, Isaac and Jacob." This is an amazing occurrence, so don't miss the implications. The Holy God who created the universe began to introduce Himself by naming the names of His people!

It's as if God is saying, "If you want to know who I AM, check out what I did in the lives of these people. The changes I've accomplished there will show you my power, my grace, my attentive care to their smallest and greatest needs." The changes in their lives authenticated the character of God, so God began to point them out as His signature. God is claiming that He is best known through His handiwork—and that we are His most significant handiwork!

When I think of the fact that God wants to show His character to the world through me, that He wants to be able to call Himself "The God of Jessica" and know that people will recognize His character in my life, it brings a whole new significance to my longing to be more like Him. I want to be sure that people see God clearly in me so that I can be His namesake, carrying His name in a way that will make Him proud.

Fill in the blank with your own name:

I AM **the God of** _____.

If God were to point to your story as one that He had touched, what evidence would there be? What aspects of your life bear God's fingerprints, showing the world that He has been at work?

Revelation, revealing who He is, is one of God's specialties. If we long to know who God is at His very core, we'll do well to pick up our end of the line and listen carefully to His voice. God speaks His name daily into our lives in a thousand different ways, not the least of which is through the work He does in you and me.

Pray About It

Look back at the times in your life when you wondered if you could trust God. What was the outcome? Take time to talk to God about the times when you've struggled to trust Him. Spend time specifically praising Him for His unchanging nature (I AM) and for His actions that have blessed your life (I will).

71

Act on It

- Make a list below of some of the interactions and relationships you've had with others this week (for example, talking to the clerk at the grocery store, eating dinner with your family, spending time with an elderly neighbor). Has God's name been glorified in the way you've treated people? Are there interactions that exemplify integrity between the name of God you carry with you and the actions you demonstrate? Are there interactions or relationships in your life that need work? What changes do you want God to help you make in the coming week?

---

1. Chaya Babu, "285 Indian girls shed 'unwanted' names," *Yahoo! News,*
   http://news.yahoo.com/285-indian-girls-shed-unwanted-names-122551876.html.

Week 2
VIDEO VIEWER GUIDE

We often _____ _____ the _____ that people speak over us.

"No wonder his name is _____, for now he has _____ me twice.

First he took my rights as the firstborn, and now he has _____ my blessing."
Genesis 27:36 NLT

"Your name will no longer be Jacob, but _____, because you have _____

_____ _____ and with humans and have overcome."
Genesis 32:28 NIV

Prayer is grabbing hold of _____ . . . and inviting Him to _____

with us through the tough times.

Sometimes it takes us _____ _____ to remember that

_____ is the One who has been in control all along.

God began to call Himself the God of _____, _____, and

_____.

Our _____ declare to the world that we have _____ hold of

_____.

Week 3
Naomi

Every Name Tells a Story: L.J.

Since the day they found out they were expecting their first child, Jack and Jessica had been calling their baby L.J.—a nickname short for Little Jack or Little Jessica. When they found out little L.J. was a boy, family tradition dictated that this baby boy would be the fourth generation to carry on the family name: John McDowell Allen.

After a relatively smooth start to her pregnancy, Jessica woke up one morning feeling that something was wrong. She rushed to the hospital and found out she was in premature labor only 26 weeks along. John McDowell Allen IV was born weighing exactly two pounds, a tiny, handsome little boy. His first pictures show his parents' wedding rings slipped over his perfect little feet like ankle bracelets. With his parents' powerful love and prayers and the support of an amazing medical team, L.J. fought against the odds, but at only 17 days old he succumbed to an infection in his blood, something his tiny system just wasn't equipped to fight.

I'll never forget standing in front of a packed church, officiating at L.J.'s funeral in front of hundreds of people. Part of a funeral service is called the "Naming." In it, the pastor tries to sum up the events and experiences of a person's life, naming his or her time on earth through the contributions the individual has made. Using words to "name" L.J.'s contribution on earth made me realize how little of our lives can be measured by successes or achievements. It was amazing that one who had spent so little time on earth made such an impact on so many. In the days following the funeral, Jessica couldn't shake the feeling that this wasn't how their story was supposed to end.

A couple of months later, their grief still fresh, Jack and Jessica received a phone call from a family friend. A teenage girl who was unprepared to be a mother was expecting a baby right around the time of L.J.'s due date. Their mutual friend felt led by God to contact Jack and Jessica to see if they would consider adopting the baby girl. At first they thought it was too soon. They hadn't had time to heal from their recent loss, much less consider their future. But that night they both lay in bed unable to sleep, wondering if God might be doing something unplanned in their family, in the life of this scared teenager, and in the life of the baby girl she was carrying. By the next morning, they turned to each other willing to consider the possibility that this baby they had only heard about might be meant for them.

In just a matter of weeks, three days after L.J.'s due date, Grace Carolyn Allen was born. When Jack and Jessica arrived at the hospital and were ushered down the hall to the room where Grace was being born, they walked in to realize it was the exact room where L.J. had made his unexpected arrival just months earlier. The doctor placed the baby girl in Jack's open arms with the words "meet your daughter." The gift they received that day was a minor miracle, evidence that God was not done offering them goodness and mercy. Nothing could replace their son or minimize the impact of his life, but it was clear God was doing something amazing through their family's story. There would be new tales to tell of the joy that entered their lives through a little girl named Grace. The story of Grace is proof to all who hear it that the grace of God is still at work, even when we feel all has been lost.

Naomi's story is also marked by the hard knocks of grief and bitterness. She was sure that life was over when she lost those she loved so dearly. Watch her story carefully, though, and you'll see that her life didn't end when grief entered. God's plans to bring grace to Naomi's life were far from over. A true friend, a fresh start, and God's redeeming mercy were about to break into the darkness she felt. Grace was just around the corner.

Bethlehem - House of Bread
Naomi - PLEASANT

Moabites—
offspring of

Day 1: The Bitter Truth

Read God's Word

¹ In the days when the judges ruled, there was a famine in the land, and a man from Bethlehem in Judah, together with his wife and two sons, went to live for a while in the country of <u>Moab.</u> ² The man's name was Elimelech, his wife's name Naomi, and the names of his two sons were Mahlon and Kilion. They were Ephrathites from Bethlehem, Judah. And they went to Moab and lived there.

³ Now Elimelech, Naomi's husband, died, and she was left with her two sons. ⁴ They married Moabite women, one named Orpah and the other Ruth. After they had lived there about ten years, ⁵ both Mahlon and Kilion also died, and Naomi was left without her two sons and her husband.

⁶ When she heard in Moab that the LORD had come to the aid of his people by providing food for them, Naomi and her daughters-in-law prepared to return home from there. ⁷ With her two daughters-in-law she left the place where she had been living and set out on the road that would take them back to the land of Judah.

⁸ Then Naomi said to her two daughters-in-law, "Go back, each of you, to your mother's home. May the LORD show kindness to you, as you have shown to your dead and to me. ⁹ May the LORD grant that each of you will find rest in the home of another husband."

Then she kissed them and they wept aloud ¹⁰ and said to her, "We will go back with you to your people."

¹¹ But Naomi said, "Return home, my daughters. Why would you come with me? Am I going to have any more sons, who could become your husbands? ¹² Return home, my daughters; I am too old to have another husband. Even if I thought there was still hope for me—even if I had a husband tonight and then gave birth to sons— ¹³ would you wait until they grew up? Would you remain unmarried for them? No, my daughters. It is more bitter for me than for you, because the LORD's hand has gone out against me!"

¹⁴ At this they wept again. Then Orpah kissed her mother-in-law good-by, but Ruth clung to her.

Ruth 1:1-14

Reflect and Respond

Grief takes your breath away. My breathless moment is frozen in a memory in front of a Christmas tree at my grandmother's house. We were finishing up the last touches on decorations, presents, and dinner while waiting for my aunt and uncle and their four kids to arrive. The phone rang. My mom answered it, and I could tell it was her brother on the other line. I remember wondering why they were running late. Then I heard my mom say, "Oh, no. Oh, no," over and over again. And then finally: "Oh, I'm so sorry." My uncle and his family had arrived at their home to find their oldest son had taken his own life. He was just twenty years old.

Time stopped for me in those few seconds after the phone rang. I can remember with odd clarity the tiny details of the room, the ache and shock that I felt, and the immediate concern for my ninety-year-old grandmother, whom we'd break the news to within minutes. Our family faced a very different kind of Christmas that year, one with grief as a centerpiece, overshadowing all the plans we had made.

We often use the words "family members" to describe those who are related to us. The term *members* is also used to describe the parts of our body; arms and legs are members of a whole. When one member is badly hurt or even removed, the whole body goes into a kind of shock, feeling the pain of dis*member*ment. The same is true when those we love are taken away. Then shock and numbness give way to overwhelming pain.

Naomi's life was torn apart when she lost everything she knew and loved. In the very first verse of the book of Ruth we learn that her homeland was rocked by such severe famine that her family was forced to evacuate, becoming refugees in the neighboring country Moab. The first loss Naomi experiences is the loss of her livelihood—her own sustenance and her ability to feed her family. This led to the loss of her home, her friends, and the familiarity of all that she knew as she and her husband fled to another country with their two boys just to survive.

If these were Naomi's only losses we would feel sorry for her, but they were nothing compared to the losses yet to come.

Reread Ruth 1:3-5. What additional losses does Naomi experience?

All in a few verses Naomi loses the three most important people in her life—her husband and two sons. Her family is dismembered, torn apart.

How does Naomi react? Not surprisingly, she is grief-stricken, bitter, and angry at God. Her daughters-in-law are loyal to her and want to stay with her, even though they are grieving the losses of their own husbands. We'll learn more about their reactions tomorrow, but even with their attempts to comfort her, Naomi's reaction shows us how alone and dejected she feels.

After she returns to Bethlehem, the women in the town are so surprised to see Naomi again. They exclaim, "Can this be Naomi?" Naomi's response speaks volumes about her emotional state:

"Don't call me Naomi," she told them. "Call me Mara, because the Almighty has made my life very bitter. I went away full, but the Lord *has brought me back empty. Why call me Naomi? The* Lord *has afflicted me; the Almighty has brought misfortune upon me."*

Ruth 1:20-21

The name Naomi means "Pleasant." What is Naomi's new name, and who changes it?

What does her new name mean?

In the verses above, circle each time Naomi names God. In each of those places, underline what Naomi says God has done.

With no one left to call her "Honey," no one left to call her "Mom," Naomi decides that "Bitter" is the name that best applies to her current identity. She lets the grief take over and name her with heartache.

Naomi's reaction isn't that surprising, really. How can we blame her for holding God responsible for the avalanche of tragedies she endured? In Elisabeth Kübler-Ross's famous work on the stages of grief, anger is a normal and common stage.[1] When there's no easy explanation or person to blame, God is often the target for our anger.

Reread Ruth 1:13. How does Naomi think God feels toward her?

Is there a time when Naomi's new name, "Bitter," applied to your life?

Have you ever turned your anger, blame, or bitterness toward God?

How did you handle it? How have those feelings changed over time?

The book of Psalms is a textbook of human emotions. If you ever feel alone in your struggles or that no one else has ever felt the way you do, a search of the psalms reveals that every feeling a person could express has been documented there.

Take a moment to look up these psalms where people struggled honestly with their feelings toward God. Quickly scan each passage and write down two or three of the strongest emotions you find in each one.

Psalm 22:1-2

Psalm 44:23-24

Psalm 88

Are any of these emotions surprising to you? Why or why not?

Why do you think they are included in Holy Scripture?

The psalms give us a picture of familiarity and freedom where our relationship with God is concerned. When you feel like pouring out your heart to God—even if your emotions are negative, you can take heart that God has heard all of it before. You can tell Him anything. If you're experiencing anger or bitterness toward God like Naomi did, you can talk to Him about it. God can take it. We never have to gloss things over in prayer, to be afraid of God's reaction, or to try to hide our negative feelings from Him.

Read Romans 8:35-39.

List below the things that cannot separate us from God's love as spelled out in these verses. Write the word "NOTHING" in bold letters across your list of things that can separate us from God.

Now list the things in your own life that may seem like obstacles to God's love but can never separate you from Him. Include your own feelings of anger, bitterness, depression, or sadness. Again, write the word "NOTHING" across your list of things that can separate you from His love.

> We can't be truly close to God in good times unless we are truly transparent with Him in bad times as well.

God wants to know our hearts and have us express ourselves honestly. As with achieving intimacy in any healthy human relationship, we can't be truly close to God in good times unless we are truly transparent with Him in bad times as well. If you're wondering how God reacts when His people accuse Him of sending them pain and punishment, we will explore that in Day 4 as we continue reading about Naomi's life. For now, know that instead of turning away from her in her grief or leaving her to stew in her own bitterness, God continued to offer her His grace and love. Even if we turn our backs on God, we can be assured that He never turns His back on us.

We will see that Scripture never condemns Naomi's anger at God and that God doesn't withhold any future goodness or blessing from her life just because she was angry with Him. Thankfully, there's a lot more to Naomi's story than this first chapter! But she's already taught us an important lesson. It's OK to be honest with God. In fact, He invites us to share our deepest struggles with Him. He wants to be part of both the good and bad parts of our life. When we're feeling discouraged, it's important to remember there are still many chapters to be written in our own stories as well.

When I remember the details of the Christmas now frozen in grief in my mind, I remember not just the shock or the odd details that stuck in my memory. I also remember, looking back, that God was there with us in that moment. That very word, *remember*, means "to put back together." Our members may be torn from us by grief in a moment, but God walks with us through the difficult moments, hours, years that follow, helping us put the pieces of our hearts back together so we can breathe again. When we feel lost or forgotten, God remembers us.

Do you have a moment that is frozen in time by grief, when you received bad news or learned you had lost someone dear to you? What are your strongest memories of that moment?

Looking back, can you see how God was present with you in that moment or the time that followed?

Although our moments of tragedy and grief often seem frozen in time, the good news is that life does continue once they have passed. It's a good thing—for Naomi and for us—that there's always more story to be written.

Pray About It

As you pray with your Bible open to Romans 8:35-39, reword these verses by inserting descriptions of your own experiences. Thank God that He is bigger than all you struggle with and that nothing will separate you from His love.

Act on It

- Reach out to someone who is grieving. If you know someone who has recently lost a loved one, send a note of condolence and encouragement.

- Think back to those who have suffered losses a year or two years ago. Although the memory may seem far away for you, it may still be very fresh for those closest to the person. Reach out to them with a call, e-mail, or letter, letting them know you remember their grief.

Day 2: Covenant Friendship

Read God's Word

¹⁵ *"Look," said Naomi, "your sister-in-law is going back to her people and her gods. Go back with her."*
¹⁶ *But Ruth replied, "Don't urge me to leave you or to turn back from you. Where you go I will go, and where you stay I will stay. Your people will be my people and your*

God my God. ¹⁷ Where you die I will die, and there I will be buried. May the LORD deal with me, be it ever so severely, if anything but death separates you and me." ¹⁸ When Naomi realized that Ruth was determined to go with her, she stopped urging her.

Ruth 1:15-18

¹ After David had finished talking with Saul, Jonathan became one in spirit with David, and he loved him as himself. ² From that day Saul kept David with him and did not let him return home to his family. ³ And Jonathan made a covenant with David because he loved him as himself. ⁴ Jonathan took off the robe he was wearing and gave it to David, along with his tunic, and even his sword, his bow and his belt.

1 Samuel 18:1-4

Reflect and Respond

I drove my little, two-door Ford across the country, packed with all my most treasured possessions. I was leaving my home state and enrolling in four years of seminary far from everyone I knew. I felt grownup, adventurous, and more than a little lonely.

With all of my closest friends hours away, I worried that I would be lost in a sea of new people. Who would appreciate my quirky sense of humor? Who would comfort me when I was homesick? As usual, I shouldn't have worried so much.

It was in the middle of my first week in my new surroundings that I met Tina. During orientation exercises new students participated in activities to help us meet new friends and feel a little less lost. During one activity, when someone shouted out a question, we were supposed to gather in circles with others who had things in common with us. Who had birthdays in the same month? I was in a circle full of Aprils. Who had the same color eyes? I was staring into a circle of greens. But then came the question: How many people were in the family you grew up in? There I was, alone in the middle of the other circles, holding up two fingers. I had grown up an only child raised by a single mom. Were there no other "twos" out there to join me? Suddenly, from somewhere in the crowd, came Tina, holding up two fingers to match mine, grinning as if she was just as relieved as me to find someone to circle up with. We became our own little circle of two.

Tina was also an only child, raised by a wonderful single mom like mine. We quickly figured out that we had a lot more in common. We became best friends and soon were roommates, too.

The years that we were roommates were some of the most joyful and most difficult of my life. During those years God was doing spiritual heart surgery on me, revealing and correcting some of my deepest flaws and unhealthy patterns in relationships, but He also was confirming again and again that He loved me and was calling me to serve Him in ministry. Through the good and the bad moments of those years, Tina was there for me. She had an uncanny way of knowing when I had a bad day and recognizing when I needed a serious listening ear or a goofy joke to cheer me up.

In the years since we lived together, Tina and I have logged lots of hours of phone conversations. We developed an ability to recognize each other's voices on the phone instantly. Instead of an introduction, the one calling would just start the conversation by saying simply, "It's me," and then launching right into conversation.

"It's me" has also come to mean "you can tell me anything," "you can be yourself with me," and "I will love you and be your friend no matter what you're going through."

If one of us begins to doubt that we can share our fears or failures, if we hesitate to disclose something painful or revealing, the other just responds, "Hey. It's me." Feeling comforted by those words, the other one will inevitably continue.

That kind of friendship, the kind that sustains us in the highest and lowest points of life, is a gift from God. God sends people into our lives as His agents, His instruments, to show us what unconditional love feels like. We can't expect our friends to be perfect, but we can expect to find signs of how God loves us in the love of other people.

Although the central figure of our story this week is Naomi, the book of the Bible that contains her story is named for her daughter-in-law Ruth. In Ruth 1, Naomi gains a gift like no other in the friendship of Ruth. Ruth's name, in fact, means "Friend." These women have been through both joy and grief together, and when Naomi decides to return to her homeland, she urges both of her daughters-in-law to return to their own families. One of them, Orpah, decides to return to her parents, but Ruth refuses to go back.

Her powerful and beautiful words have become classic poetry:

"Where you go I will go, and where you stay I will stay. Your people will be my people and your God my God. Where you die I will die, and there I will be buried. May the LORD deal with me, be it ever so severely, if anything but death separates you and me." When Naomi realized that Ruth was determined to go with her, she stopped urging her.

Ruth 1:16-18

> God sends people into our lives as His agents, His instruments, to show us what unconditional love feels like.

What does Ruth pledge to Naomi?

Your _____ will be my _____.

Your _____ (will be) my _____.

Where you _____ I will _____.

What does Ruth say to convey the earnestness of her pledge?

With these words, Ruth is forming a covenant friendship with Naomi. Their connection as a family was severed by the death of Ruth's husband, Naomi's son. Ruth's covenant reinstates the bonds of family between them. Stronger than a contract, a covenant has at its center the God they will both worship and follow. They'll need God's strength to carry them through the difficult days ahead.

God often provides us with strength in a very real and physical way by providing us with each other for support. The spiritual is made real in the tangible, loving support of the people of God in our lives.

Reread Ruth 1:15. What does Naomi say Orpah is returning to?

Even though her family religion and background were probably the same as Orpah's, Ruth promises to worship Naomi's God—the one true God. What do you think this promise meant to Naomi?

Ruth's poetic words bind her in covenant friendship to Naomi, but they also bind her to Naomi's God. They are not just words of camaraderie; they are words of conversion. Where once Naomi and Ruth had shared common love and common grief, now they shared a common faith. While it's important for us to reach out and create friendships with nonbelievers, it's also important for our souls to nurture friendships with others who have faith in Jesus Christ.

How might having common faith have helped Ruth and Naomi support one another?

Ruth and Naomi faced the common struggle of grief for those they loved and lost. This obstacle strengthened their friendship by giving them a deep understanding for one another's pain.

Have you ever felt connected to someone because you faced a common struggle in life? If so, how were you able to help each other with that struggle?

Each of us starts out in life with a family of origin, the family that we are born into and raised in. We end up in life in a family of destination, the family we may marry into, give birth to, or end up living with as adults. There is another kind of family called a family choice. These are people who may have no blood relation to us but may become as close as or closer than family. This kind of friendship can bring us some of the greatest joy and comfort we will ever experience in life.

Read Proverbs 18:24. What does this verse imply about covenant friendship and family of choice?

Ruth made an alliance of friendship with Naomi that went beyond their bloodlines. She chose to reject ties with family members in order to support and protect a friend. Covenant friendship often runs deeper than ties with relatives.

Have you ever had to reject the beliefs or habits of your family? If so, were there friends whose lives and decisions you identified with more closely than your family ties?

Are there people in your life whom you have made your family of choice (those who are not related to you but whom you treat like family)? If so, how have those friendships sustained you in life?

One of God's greatest gifts to us is the gift of friendship. Through our friends, we receive God's love, kindness, laughter, and grace through a human delivery system. As you reflect on the friendships you've treasured in life, remember the source, the Giver of all good gifts.

One who has unreliable friends soon comes to ruin, but there is a friend who sticks closer than a brother.
Proverbs 18:24

Pray About It

List below the people whose friendship has had a significant impact on your life. Can you see God at work in bringing such wonderful people across your path?

Acknowledge that each of these persons came into your life as a gift from God. Say a prayer of thanksgiving, giving God thanks for sending you these people as instruments of His friendship and love for you.

Act on It

Beside each description, write the name or initials of someone in your life who fits this category:

- **Someone who has been a covenant friend to you. _____**
  Take time to reach out to your covenant friend and let him or her know how meaningful the friendship has been to you.

- **Someone you'd like to develop a deeper and more meaningful friendship with. _____**
  Plan an outing or activity with this person to develop stronger ties.

- **Someone who needs a friend. _____**
  List below ways you can support and show care for this person.

Day 3: Love in Action

Read God's Word

[1] *Now Naomi had a relative on her husband's side, from the clan of Elimelech, a man of standing, whose name was Boaz.*

² *And Ruth the Moabitess said to Naomi, "Let me go to the fields and pick up the leftover grain behind anyone in whose eyes I find favor."*

Naomi said to her, "Go ahead, my daughter." ³ *So she went out and began to glean in the fields behind the harvesters. As it turned out, she found herself working in a field belonging to Boaz, who was from the clan of Elimelech.*

⁴ *Just then Boaz arrived from Bethlehem and greeted the harvesters, "The LORD be with you!"*

"The LORD bless you!" they called back.

⁵ *Boaz asked the foreman of his harvesters, "Whose young woman is that?"*

⁶ *The foreman replied, "She is the Moabitess who came back from Moab with Naomi.* ⁷ *She said, 'Please let me glean and gather among the sheaves behind the harvesters.' She went into the field and has worked steadily from morning till now, except for a short rest in the shelter."* Leftovers for Widows + children

⁸ *So Boaz said to Ruth, "My daughter, listen to me. Don't go and glean in another field and don't go away from here. Stay here with my servant girls.* ⁹ *Watch the field where the men are harvesting, and follow along after the girls. I have told the men not to touch you. And whenever you are thirsty, go and get a drink from the water jars the men have filled."*

¹⁰ *At this, she bowed down with her face to the ground. She exclaimed, "Why have I found such favor in your eyes that you notice me —a foreigner?"*

¹¹ *Boaz replied, "I've been told all about what you have done for your mother-in-law since the death of your husband—how you left your father and mother and your homeland and came to live with a people you did not know before.* ¹² *May the LORD repay you for what you have done. May you be richly rewarded by the LORD, the God of Israel, under whose wings you have come to take refuge."*

¹³ *"May I continue to find favor in your eyes, my lord," she said. "You have given me comfort and have spoken kindly to your servant—though I do not have the standing of one of your servant girls."*

¹⁴ *At mealtime Boaz said to her, "Come over here. Have some bread and dip it in the wine vinegar."*

When she sat down with the harvesters, he offered her some roasted grain. She ate all she wanted and had some left over. ¹⁵ *As she got up to glean, Boaz gave orders to his men, "Even if she gathers among the sheaves, don't embarrass her.* ¹⁶ *Rather, pull out some stalks for her from the bundles and leave them for her to pick up, and don't rebuke her."*

¹⁷ *So Ruth gleaned in the field until evening. Then she threshed the barley she had gathered, and it amounted to about an ephah.* ¹⁸ *She carried it back to town, and her mother-in-law saw how much she had gathered. Ruth also brought out and gave her what she had left over after she had eaten enough.*

¹⁹ *Her mother-in-law asked her, "Where did you glean today? Where did you work? Blessed be the man who took notice of you!"*

Then Ruth told her mother-in-law about the one at whose place she had been working. "The name of the man I worked with today is Boaz," she said.

[20] *"The LORD bless him!" Naomi said to her daughter-in-law. "He has not stopped showing his kindness to the living and the dead." She added, "That man is our close relative; he is one of our kinsman-redeemers."*

[21] *Then Ruth the Moabitess said, "He even said to me, 'Stay with my workers until they finish harvesting all my grain.'"*

[22] *Naomi said to Ruth her daughter-in-law, "It will be good for you, my daughter, to go with his girls, because in someone else's field you might be harmed."*

[23] *So Ruth stayed close to the servant girls of Boaz to glean until the barley and wheat harvests were finished. And she lived with her mother-in-law.*

Ruth 2:1-23

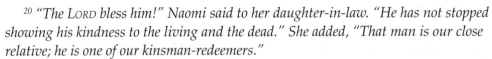

Reflect and Respond

Rachel sat across a table from me at a coffee shop, crying. Her life was in shambles. Her promising future had taken a detour halfway through college when she got pregnant and moved back home to have a baby. The baby's father wanted no part of supporting them or being part of their lives. A couple of years later she met what she thought was the man of her dreams. After a whirlwind courtship, they married and became an instant family with lots of hope for the future. Now, only a few months later, they were separated and headed for divorce. She was back to living with her parents and relying on their help while she searched in vain for a job that could support her and her daughter, but daycare costs were greater than any salary she qualified for.

"I just don't know what to do anymore!" Rachel told me. "I sit at home and wonder about my future. I can't seem to figure it out, and my thoughts just go in circles!"

After listening to her talk for almost an hour, I made a simple suggestion: "Why not come with us on Saturday to the Habitat for Humanity build? There's nursery care at the church for your little girl, and I think you might enjoy getting out with other people." She looked at me like I was crazy. She was expecting me to help solve her problems. Why was I suggesting she help fix someone else's?

Naomi and Ruth's story holds some insight into Rachel's situation. In the very first chapter of Naomi's story (Ruth 1), we learned how she dealt with her grief and loss by becoming bitter and lashing out at God. Scripture doesn't judge her reaction to tragedy, and neither do we. After all, anger and depression are very understandable and normal stages of grief. But in time they need to become just that, *stages* that we move through on our way to other parts of our journey rather than places where we stay stuck. But how do we find a way to move on?

Ruth experienced the same kinds of loss that we see in Naomi's story. She also was grieving the loss of her husband, as well as her father-in-law and brother-in-law. She had just left her homeland, including her family and friends and every-thing familiar and comforting to her, just as Naomi had done after the famine. Ruth must have experienced the same pain and tears that Naomi did. She may have even gone through similar stages of anger and depression. But in chapter 2, Ruth's grief begins to take on a different shape.

Reread Ruth 2:2. What does Ruth request as soon as she and Naomi return to Bethlehem?

What do we learn about Ruth's work ethic in Ruth 2:7?

When they arrived in Bethlehem, Ruth found herself in a desperate situation. In that particular time and culture, the male members of the household would work to supply food and shelter for their family. Ruth and Naomi had no one to provide for them, a situation that made their grief and loss seem even more hopeless. If no one took action on their behalf, it was possible that they could starve or be forced to beg on the streets.

Instead of wallowing or waiting for someone else to take responsibility, Ruth channeled her grief, worry, and anxiety into action. With Naomi's blessing, she went to the fields each day to glean—to gather the leftovers the harvesters had dropped. She worked tirelessly until sundown, and we're told she worked the entire season until the harvest had finished. Ruth's initiative and determination saved her life and Naomi's, and it set into motion a course of events that would change their lives forever.

Read Isaiah 6:8. God is calling for someone to step up and take action. What is Isaiah's response? Can you hear Ruth making a similar declaration?

When you've been faced with circumstances that overwhelmed you, how did you respond? Do you identify more with Naomi's reaction of being rendered inactive, frozen by her circumstances, or Ruth's "get-up-and-go" tendency to take care of it herself?

Then I heard the voice of the Lord saying, "Whom shall I send? And who will go for us?" Isaiah 6:8

89

If we are feeling stressed and overwhelmed by the circumstances of our own lives, it sometimes helps to look outside ourselves to the needs of others. That seems counterintuitive. If our resources are scarce and our lives frazzled, shouldn't we stay focused on solving our own problems? Isn't it true that "God helps those who help themselves"? Actually, that phrase is nowhere to be found in the Bible. Instead, Scripture offers us a different prescription.

Read Philippians 2:3-4. Write verse 4 below:

This is a remedy best applied to our own wounds, not to others. When someone is struggling or in pain, a listening ear is almost always the best help we can offer. But if we apply this medicine to our own hurts, it often turns out that our example of caring for the needs of others, even when our needs are great, can inspire those who are watching to do the same. That was certainly true in Ruth's case. Her goodness and hard work were noticed and rewarded.

First, Boaz, the owner of the fields in which Ruth worked each day, noticed her determination. He perceived that Ruth was a remarkable young woman. He saw that she wasn't wallowing in self-pity or waiting for someone to take care of her problems for her. And her take-charge attitude inspired Boaz to help her succeed.

Reread Ruth 2:5-16. List the things that Boaz does for Ruth out of kindness.

1.

2.

3.

4.

5.

Why does he tell her he is doing these things (vv. 11-12)?

When Ruth returned home with an amount of barley that was obviously more than she could have gathered under normal circumstances, Naomi knew something was up. Ruth obviously had help.

Ruth's heart of service toward Naomi inspired Boaz to help her. And in turn, watching Ruth's tireless hard work and kindness and learning of Boaz's acts of compassion helped wake Naomi from her fog of grief. After her bitterness and depression had kept her frozen and immobile for so long, something in Naomi began to melt. Her sense of hope began to return. She saw Ruth's plan of action to keep them alive and she began to come up with a plan of her own. And that's when things really started to turn around for Ruth and Naomi.

Naomi knew that she and Ruth couldn't live on leftover wheat forever, and so she put into action a plan so controversial it had to be done under the cover of darkness. She planned to get Boaz to marry Ruth and restore their family to financial health and standing in the community (a plan we will explore in detail tomorrow as we study chapter 3). And her plan worked!

- Ruth acted with selflessness, serving Naomi.
- Boaz acted with integrity, serving and protecting Ruth.
- Naomi came up with a plan that had daring audacity, one that would serve to reward Ruth for her kindness and ensure a future with hope for all of them.

Think of a way you have seen people help others by acting:

with audacity (like Naomi's plan)

with integrity (like Boaz's response)

with submission and selflessness (like Ruth's actions)

Peeking ahead to the happy ending of the story, we find that when Boaz and Ruth marry and have their first child, they name him Obed. Obed's name means "Servant." This may seem an unusual name for the son of the boss, the landowner who had servants working for him. Why name their child "Servant"? The clue to that mystery can be found by examining the heart of Obed's parents and grandmother. They had servants' hearts, thinking of others before themselves, not unlike the One who would come much later in their family tree.

Read Matthew 1:5, 16. Who is the ultimate offspring of this family?

What does Mark 10:45 say about Him?

But even the Son of Man did not come to be served, but to serve, and to give his life as a ransom for many.
Mark 10:45

Rachel did come with us on the Habitat for Humanity build that Saturday. The offer of a Saturday of free babysitting was more than a single mom could resist! She had never worked with construction tools before, but she was able to hammer in a few nails in sheetrock, help prepare lunch, and bring water to other workers on a very hot Texas day. Best of all she met Rosario, the single mom for whom we were helping build the house. Rosario had a sad story of her own, but there she was working alongside us, excited to help finish the first house she and her four kids would get to call home. Hearing Rosario's story and watching her work so hard alongside those who had come to help her really had an effect on Rachel. Her own story seemed less overwhelming as she focused on someone else's needs for a few hours. When she returned home that day, nothing in her circumstances had changed, but something in her outlook was definitely shifting in a new direction.

Have you ever felt overwhelmed by grief, hopelessness, or depression? What helped you emerge from that cycle?

We worship a God who serves. He came to earth not as a magnificent king but as a lowly rabbi. When the opportunity presented itself for Him to sit back and be catered to at His last dinner on earth, He instead took the role of servant, washing the feet of those who followed Him. That role of serving those He loves is one He is still acting on today.

Pray About It

Jesus, thank You that instead of insisting on glory and riches, You took on the form of a servant. You didn't have to humble Yourself and look to serve our greatest needs, but You did, and I am grateful. Make me more like You. Make me a servant. Change my heart and help me to change Your world. Amen.

Act on It

- Find a way to serve this week. It might be something as simple as spontaneously loaning a helping hand to someone while you are out and about, to taking a meal or making a visit to someone who is ill or shut in, to giving several hours to a service opportunity in your local church or community.

Day 4: Undercover God

Read God's Word

¹ One day Naomi her mother-in-law said to her, "My daughter, should I not try to find a home for you, where you will be well provided for? ² Is not Boaz, with whose servant girls you have been, a kinsman of ours? Tonight he will be winnowing barley on the threshing floor. ³ Wash and perfume yourself, and put on your best clothes. Then go down to the threshing floor, but don't let him know you are there until he has finished eating and drinking. ⁴ When he lies down, note the place where he is lying. Then go and uncover his feet and lie down. He will tell you what to do."

⁵ "I will do whatever you say," Ruth answered. ⁶ So she went down to the threshing floor and did everything her mother-in-law told her to do.

⁷ When Boaz had finished eating and drinking and was in good spirits, he went over to lie down at the far end of the grain pile. Ruth approached quietly, uncovered his feet and lay down. ⁸ In the middle of the night something startled the man, and he turned and discovered a woman lying at his feet.

⁹ "Who are you?" he asked.

"I am your servant Ruth," she said. "Spread the corner of your garment over me, since you are a kinsman-redeemer."

¹⁰ "The LORD bless you, my daughter," he replied. "This kindness is greater than that which you showed earlier: You have not run after the younger men, whether rich or poor. ¹¹ And now, my daughter, don't be afraid. I will do for you all you ask. All my fellow townsmen know that you are a woman of noble character. ¹² Although it is true that I am near of kin, there is a kinsman-redeemer nearer than I. ¹³ Stay here for the night, and in the morning if he wants to redeem, good; let him redeem. But if he is not willing, as surely as the LORD lives I will do it. Lie here until morning."

¹⁴ So she lay at his feet until morning, but got up before anyone could be recognized; and he said, "Don't let it be known that a woman came to the threshing floor."

¹⁵ He also said, "Bring me the shawl you are wearing and hold it out." When she did so, he poured into it six measures of barley and put it on her. Then he went back to town.

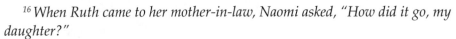

16 When Ruth came to her mother-in-law, Naomi asked, "How did it go, my daughter?"

Then she told her everything Boaz had done for her 17 and added, "He gave me these six measures of barley, saying, 'Don't go back to your mother-in-law empty-handed.'"

18 Then Naomi said, "Wait, my daughter, until you find out what happens. For the man will not rest until the matter is settled today."

Ruth 3:1-18

1 Meanwhile Boaz went up to the town gate and sat there. When the kinsman-redeemer he had mentioned came along, Boaz said, "Come over here, my friend, and sit down." So he went over and sat down.

2 Boaz took ten of the elders of the town and said, "Sit here," and they did so. 3 Then he said to the kinsman-redeemer, "Naomi, who has come back from Moab, is selling the piece of land that belonged to our brother Elimelech. 4 I thought I should bring the matter to your attention and suggest that you buy it in the presence of these seated here and in the presence of the elders of my people. If you will redeem it, do so. But if you will not, tell me, so I will know. For no one has the right to do it except you, and I am next in line."

"I will redeem it," he said.

5 Then Boaz said, "On the day you buy the land from Naomi and from Ruth the Moabitess, you acquire the dead man's widow, in order to maintain the name of the dead with his property."

6 At this, the kinsman-redeemer said, "Then I cannot redeem it because I might endanger my own estate. You redeem it yourself. I cannot do it."

7 (Now in earlier times in Israel, for the redemption and transfer of property to become final, one party took off his sandal and gave it to the other. This was the method of legalizing transactions in Israel.)

8 So the kinsman-redeemer said to Boaz, "Buy it yourself." And he removed his sandal.

9 Then Boaz announced to the elders and all the people, "Today you are witnesses that I have bought from Naomi all the property of Elimelech, Kilion and Mahlon. 10 I have also acquired Ruth the Moabitess, Mahlon's widow, as my wife, in order to maintain the name of the dead with his property, so that his name will not disappear from among his family or from the town records. Today you are witnesses!"

11 Then the elders and all those at the gate said, "We are witnesses. May the LORD make the woman who is coming into your home like Rachel and Leah, who together built up the house of Israel. May you have standing in Ephrathah and be famous in Bethlehem. 12 Through the offspring the LORD gives you by this young woman, may your family be like that of Perez, whom Tamar bore to Judah."

13 So Boaz took Ruth and she became his wife. Then he went to her, and the LORD enabled her to conceive, and she gave birth to a son. 14 The women said to Naomi: "Praise be to the LORD, who this day has not left you without a kinsman-redeemer. May he become famous throughout Israel! ¹⁵ *He will renew your life and sustain you in your old age. For your daughter-in-law, who loves you and who is better to you than seven sons, has given him birth."*

¹⁶ *Then Naomi took the child, laid him in her lap and cared for him.* ¹⁷ *The women living there said, "Naomi has a son." And they named him Obed. He was the father of Jesse, the father of David.*

Ruth 4:1-17

Reflect and Respond

I know when I read the Bible I'm supposed to feel holier, wiser, closer to God. But I have to admit that sometimes, while I'm reading some of the greatest stories in Scripture, I actually feel a little jealous. I'm sure that's not a very saintly response, but I can't help it. I confess I have miracle envy. And I like to eat cookie dough ice cream right out of the carton. Bless me, for I have sinned.

When I read the awesome stories of how God worked in people's lives in powerful and visible ways, I find myself wishing that God would show up and work in the same way in my life. Sometimes I think my faith would be stronger and my doubts weaker if I could just witness the kinds of events that people in the Bible were able to witness up close and personal.

But then I remember that even those who saw miracles with their own eyes didn't always believe. Moses still doubted his ability to lead even after God spelled it out through the burning bush. The disciples had trouble understanding Jesus' messages and believing in His power even after learning from Him and seeing Him perform miracles with their own eyes. They heard Jesus explain that He would die and rise from the dead, and yet they still didn't understand what was going on when it happened. If the people who had front row seats to God's visible miracles didn't get it, what makes me think I would be different?

Read about the response of one eyewitness to Jesus' life and miracles in John 20:24-31.

What did he say to Jesus in verse 25?

"Unless I _____ . . . I will not _____."
(NIV)

Have you ever told God something similar? That you won't believe until you can see or touch something tangible?

95

Who does Jesus say is blessed in verse 29? Does that include you?

When I start to feel a little underprivileged compared to those who witnessed God's miraculous works firsthand, it helps me to read Naomi's story. When she felt lost and alone in her grief, she didn't see any burning bushes or get any celestial words of comfort. God didn't part a Red Sea in order for her to travel home, He didn't raise her loved ones from the dead, and He didn't miraculously multiply anything to feed her and her widowed daughter-in-law. God's works are invisible here, and yet God's presence is certainly felt throughout this book.

Read 2 Corinthians 4:17-18. What are we to fix our eyes on?

> Many of the happy coincidences in life are actually God working behind the scenes for our good.

One of my favorite phrases in Naomi's story is found toward the beginning of chapter 2. It's actually a turning point in the story, flipping a switch from tragedy to hope: "As it turned out, [Ruth] found herself working in a field belonging to Boaz, who was from the clan of Elimelech" (v. 3). The phrase "As it turned out" could also be translated "As luck would have it."

This is one of the greatest understatements in the Bible! The fact that Ruth "coincidentally" ended up in the fields belonging to Boaz, the one person in all of Bethlehem with the position and compassion to help Ruth and Naomi, is what brings about the eventual happy ending for all of the members of this family.

"As luck would have it . . . " "Luck" would have to be smart enough, loving enough, intentional enough, and powerful enough to make sure that of all the fields surrounding Bethlehem, Ruth would find herself in the one place that could turn this story around and drastically change her future—and Naomi's—forever. Luck often gets credit for the things that God is doing behind the scenes.

When we experience something that is inexplicably helpful, timely, or uncanny in the way it specifically meets our needs, we often refer to it as a coincidence. I believe there are fewer true coincidences than we think. As Christians, we need to come to recognize that many of the happy coincidences in life are actually God working behind the scenes for our good. I've heard others refer to them as "God-incidences"—a way of shifting our gratitude from the happenstance forces of fate to the intentional goodness of God.

To Naomi's credit, she recognized right away that God was at work. She was quick to blame God when things went wrong, but now she was quick to praise Him when she saw something happening that she knew was too wonderfully planned to be coincidental.

Read Ruth 2:20 and answer the following questions.

What is Naomi's reaction when she first learns whose fields Ruth has ended up working in?

How is her tone different here from what it has been up to this point in the story?

Where does she place the credit?

How is this different from her reaction in Ruth 1:19-21?

Naomi's realization that God was working for good on her behalf was a turning point for her. She stopped focusing on the negative past and began to work for positive change for a future for her and Ruth.

In yesterday's reading we saw how Ruth recognized that if she wanted something to change, she would have to take action. Today we see that all along God has been acting and working behind the scenes. Those two things together are often a recipe for miracles in our lives. We need both God's powerful action in our lives and our own initiative, joining with Him to work for good. Depending on one or the other ignores the fact that God so clearly wants to work in partnership with us in this world. He is at work for our good, and He wants us to join Him.

Write Romans 8:28 below:

How do you see this principle at work in Naomi's life?

In yours?

In chapter 1, Naomi tells the women who greet her on her way back into Bethlehem not to call her Naomi (Pleasant) anymore, but to call her Mara (Bitter). Then at the very end of the book those same women praise God for the circumstances He has used to bring her joy.

Reread Ruth 4:12-17. Which of the two names that Naomi has gone by do the women of the village use when they address her in Ruth 4:17? Pleasant or Bitter?

God loves to work in secret and see if we can uncover His goodness.

God loves to work in secret and see if we can uncover His goodness. He is working not only for our good, for each of our small stories, but also for the good of His creation—for the Big Story that is always greater than anything we can wrap our minds around. While this is Naomi's story (in a book with Ruth's name on the cover), it is so much bigger than about just Naomi's individual life. What appears to be a happy ending for her is really a beginning of a new and grander story. The grandson whose birth marks the end of her story here, Obed, will grow up to be the grandfather of King David, the most influential king Israel ever knew. And as we saw yesterday Jesus Himself, the long-awaited Messiah, eventually would descend from his lineage.

Ruth's seemingly accidental choice of fields to glean in is one of many God-incidences that had to happen to make the joyful outcome of this story possible.

Scan the four short chapters of Ruth and note below all of the positive things that just seem to "happen" to restore Naomi and Ruth to wholeness, stability, and joy.

There are many places in Scripture where God is at work even though His presence is hidden from plain sight. Read the following passages and note how God is at work in each.

John 20:13-17

Luke 24:30-32

Matthew 24:31-40

Hebrews 13:2

Can you think of other examples in Scripture?

God is using circumstance, or coincidence, or God-incidence—whatever we choose to call it—to be sure His amazing plans and purposes are accomplished in the long run. We don't have to be jealous of those who witnessed bona fide miracles in Scripture, because God is at work in and around us all the time. We simply need to learn to see.

Pray about It

Think back to the times you've said something like "we were fortunate that . . ." or "as luck would have it . . ." or "wasn't it a happy coincidence that...."

List below things that have happened in your life that may have been God working undercover.

Thank God for the times and ways He has worked behind the scenes in your life—both the things you have recognized and the things you aren't even aware of.

Act on It

- Be on the lookout for God-incidences this week. Keep a list—here or in a journal—of ways that God may be at work undercover in your life. Write down even the smallest possibilities, since sometimes it takes time to see God's plans develop.

Ways God might be at work undercover in my life:

Day 5: Revelation: Kinsman-Redeemer

Read God's Word

¹⁹ Her mother-in-law asked her, "Where did you glean today? Where did you work? Blessed be the man who took notice of you!"

Then Ruth told her mother-in-law about the one at whose place she had been working. "The name of the man I worked with today is Boaz," she said.

²⁰ "The Lord bless him! " Naomi said to her daughter-in-law. "He has not stopped showing his kindness to the living and the dead." She added, "That man is our close relative; he is one of our kinsman-redeemers."

Ruth 2:19-20

Reflect and Respond

When we named our daughter Katherine Juliet, friends commented that her name sounded like royalty, or at least like someone out of Shakespeare. The Kate most talked about in the news in the last couple of years is royalty, a real-life princess: the beautifully poised young woman who will probably be the next queen of England. I've kept some pictures of the wedding of Kate and Prince William, which took place while I was pregnant with our little Kate, so that she can see them someday. Watching that royal wedding took so many women back to the dreams of their childhood, like watching a real-life fairy tale.

Now that I have a daughter, I do feel a certain excitement about a future that includes watching movies about princesses and playing dress up with gowns, pearls, and tiaras. As a girl I loved all the Disney princess movies, the ones that told basically the same story: a princess, beautiful but helpless, finds herself in a dangerous situation and needs someone to rescue her. A prince, of the charming variety, comes along and is enraptured by her loveliness. He fights the battle she needs fought. She is overwhelmed with gratitude, falls into his arms, and they live happily ever after.

But along with nostalgia for the stories I loved as a little girl, I also have a growing wariness about these fairy tales. I'm starting to realize that although those stories captured my imagination and gave me some of my first dreams of romance, they also did me a great disservice. They planted a desire in me for someone to come along when I was in distress, rescue me from my reality, and carry me away to happily-ever-after.

100

I know it's not Walt Disney's fault, but I spent a great deal of time and energy looking for that prince, the one who would make my life complete. It turned out that every man I met fell short of that expectation (not to mention bringing with them some problems of their own!), and I was left lonely and confused to begin the search again. It would be hard for me to overemphasize how much that obsession threw me off balance, causing me to over-focus on having a man in my life, charming or not. Because of it I neglected friendships and family relationships, missed lots of opportunities to rely on Jesus, and underestimated my ability to solve my own problems and progress unassisted toward my own happily-ever-after.

Fairy tales encourage us to place our hope in fantasies of rescue and romance. Where does Scripture encourage us to place our hope?

Isaiah 40:31

Jeremiah 17:7-8

I'm not alone. Telling a friend about the new man in her life, one woman said, "We met after my divorce, and he was my savior." Really? I'm sure he's great, but put anyone but Jesus on that particular pedestal and he's sure to fall right off.

I want to offer Kate a story big enough to build real dreams on. I want her to dream about a story that will capture her imagination and her longings, but I also want those longings to be ones that will actually be fulfilled. I want her to know that yes, she does need a Savior, and that He is the One who can provide the kind of rescue we *all* need.

I don't mind if Kate wants to dress up as Cinderella or Sleeping Beauty, but I don't want her to learn those stories by heart until I have a chance to tell her another story. A true story. The story of Ruth.

Here's what I love about Ruth, the anti-princess:

- She's from the despised land of Moab (and not the chosen people of Israel), but that doesn't stop her from becoming our heroine. Just the fact that she gets the starring role means that God doesn't play favorites.
- The central relationship of her story is not a romance but a friendship between women. Our daughters need to know that friendships will be some of the strongest and most meaningful blessings in their lives, and that they should hold tightly to them, even when they think Prince Charming beckons.
- When tragedy strikes and Ruth and Naomi are left without a man to provide for them, Ruth doesn't bemoan the fact that she has no rights, or that

Those who hope [wait] in the Lord will renew their strength. They will soar on wings like eagles; they will run and not grow weary, they will walk and not be faint.
Isaiah 40:31

she could be left begging on the streets, or worse. Instead of waiting for Prince Charming to do something about her problems, she gets out and finds a solution herself, working in the fields and bringing home the bacon (or in this case, barley) to support herself and Naomi.

- When Naomi plays matchmaker between Ruth and Boaz, the wealthy owner of the field she's been working in, the two women are clearly the ones taking control of their destinies. These are women who aren't afraid to write their own fairy-tale ending.

Instead of mistaking the romantic relationship of this story for another "Prince Charming" situation, where a man rides in on a white horse to save the helpless women, let's consider the role Boaz plays in the story.

When Naomi realizes that Ruth and Boaz have become acquainted, she speaks her first positive words in the whole story after a long line of "Woe is me" negativity:

Reread Ruth 2:20. By what term does Ruth call Boaz?

In Hebrew, kinsman-redeemer is *go'el*. That title describes a role given by the law in Leviticus to a man who would help out a family member in distress by "redeeming" them. The law of Israel declared that a kinsman-redeemer was responsible to redeem a relative who had fallen on hard times and needed rescue. This was called the Levirate law.

Look up each of the following passages and describe the role of the kinsman-redeemer in each law:

Leviticus 25:25

Leviticus 25:47-49

Deuteronomy 25:5-10

This last role is why Naomi says Yahweh hasn't forgotten His kindness even to the dead. A true gentleman, a true *go'el*, would marry a widow of his closest male relative and give inheritance to those children even though they'd be

> The law of Israel declared that a kinsman-redeemer was responsible to redeem a relative who had fallen on hard times and needed rescue.

considered the children of the deceased. Though that may seem strange to us today, in Naomi's day, the kinsman-redeemer was someone highly valued by family members because they could count on him to come to the rescue when they were desperate. Besides being a human agent with responsibility to help family members, a kinsman-redeemer was also definitely an instrument of God. While the human kinsman-redeemer is working in plain sight, the true Redeemer is the one working behind the scenes. Scripture is clear about the fact that God is the ultimate Kinsman-Redeemer. Any human being who takes on that role is simply showing the world how God comes to our rescue when we need His help. Scripture uses the word *go'el* to describe God as redeemer.

Look up these verses describing God as go'el. Write any insights about the character of God that you find:

Exodus 6:6

Psalm 49:15

Isaiah 43:1

Ruth and Naomi's story makes it clear that Boaz is not the prince here. He may be the *go'el* redeeming them from a life of poverty and hunger, but God is the great *Go'el* behind the scenes, redeeming their story of grief and brokenness, bringing light where there was only darkness.

In Luke 15 we read three stories that speak to us of redemption—three stories of individuals who lose something and then recover it. In each story, the person who experienced loss never gave up searching and hoping for the return.

Read Luke 15:1-13. What is lost in each of these stories?

1.

2.

3.

In each story the stakes get higher, from 1 in 100, to 1 in 10, to 1 in 2. With each story the item lost and found gets more valuable: a sheep, a coin, and then a son, treasured from birth, given a name and a home and a family to belong to.

The third story is the best known and is often called the story of the Prodigal Son. It clearly shows God's heart as a Father aching for His children to be safe at home in close and loving relationship with Him. God is whispering to us that we are the most valuable thing in His kingdom, more valuable than a sheep or a coin; we are His children, His daughters.

In these three stories, God is showing us a Redeemer who stops at nothing to find what is lost. And He's saying: That's me! I'm the Shepherd. I'm the Coin-owner. I'm the Father. And you are the ones I seek. I will stop at nothing until you are found, redeemed, and returned home, safe and sound with me.

The romance in the book of Ruth is another story with a hidden hero. The true Redeemer peeks from behind the scenes, waiting to see if we can find Him whispering an invitation through the story. Transfixed by the happy marriage of Boaz and Ruth, we just might find ourselves caught up in our own love story, one with the Kinsman-Redeemer, who is at work to claim what is lost. He will not stop until we are found.

Let's take a closer look at how God is our Kinsman-Redeemer, our *Go'el*.

Read each passage and complete the statement that follows.

Genesis 1:27—God Created **us, which means we belonged first to Him. To redeem something means to return something to its original owner, state, or purpose. All people, whether they are aware of it or not, are God's creations, made for relationship with Him.**

Genesis 3:12-13—When Adam and Eve ate **the forbidden** fruit **, they sinned, and this separated them from God. God's plan for us to remain in close relationship with Him was thwarted in the very first generation. And in every generation and every human heart since, there has been a moment when we have decided to run away from God.**

1 John 3:1-2—Because we are God's Children **, God is our nearest relative. He lavishes on us every gift and privilege that the very best kind of human father lavishes on his children.**

Ephesians 2:13; 1 Peter 1:18-19—We have been redeemed by the blood **of Christ. He alone had the means and power to buy us back—to pay the only price acceptable for our sins. What do these two passages tell you about God's redeeming love?**

How have you seen God come to the rescue as Redeemer?

Let's be clear. Each and every one of us needs a rescuer, a Redeemer, and we will not find Him in the personal ads. He is always the One behind every earthly rescue and every romance of the truest kind. Just as He was at work in Ruth's story all along, romancing her through every circumstance and saving grace, so He is at work in each of our lives, leading us toward the one and only true happily-ever-after. Move over Snow White. This is the kind of fairy tale we can build dreams on.

Pray About It

God, thank You for the times that I named above that I've seen You come to the rescue. Help me to count on You more for my everyday needs, whether big or small. When I'm tempted to wait for rescue from a dream I've created or a story I've heard, remind me that You are the source of all help. I want to depend on You. Show me how to do that today. Amen.

Act on It

- How can you be part of God's rescue in this world? Think of situations you see that are unjust or unfair. These may be around the world or in your own backyard. Find a practical way that you can be an agent of justice and redemption today (for example, giving money to an organization that provides for the poor, volunteering at a community clinic or school, helping right some wrong that you see being done in your community).

"I know that my Redeemer [Go'el] lives, and that in the end he will stand upon the earth."
Job 19:25

---

1. Elizabeth Kübler-Ross, *On Death and Dying* (New York: MacMillan, 1969).

Week 3
VIDEO VIEWER GUIDE

When they arrived in Bethlehem, the whole town was stirred because of them, and

the women exclaimed, "Can this be Naomi?"

"Don't call me Naomi," she told them. "Call me ___Mara___ *, because the*

Almighty has made my life very ___bitter___ *. I went away full, but the*

LORD has brought me back empty. Why call me Naomi? The ___Lord___ *has*

afflicted me; the Almighty has brought misfortune upon me."

Ruth 1:19-21 NIV

We can be our own _____ _____. We can let our

_____ rob us of who we were really meant to be.

1. God's ___Intentional___ Will—God's ideal plan for us
2. God's ___Circumstantial___ Will—God's plan when circumstances are less

than ideal

3. God's ___Ultimate___ Will—God accomplishes His purposes for us

in the end without fail

Instead of being the ___villian___ in our lives when things go wrong, God is there in the circumstances ___with___ us. He has a plan to ___turn___ things around.

God's will is not defeated by ___Circumstances___.

Your ___Struggle___ is often your pathway to ___Strength___.

Naomi - Pleasant - Lovely
Bethlehem -
Elimelich - God is my King
Mahlon - headaches
Killion - finishing

Intentional Will
Circumstantial Will
Ultimate Will

Book Les!:
The Will Of GOD FOR GOOD

Week 4
Daniel

Every Name Tells a Story: Hiyab

From the time she was a teenager, Erika knew that she wanted to adopt a child someday. "Every kid needs a family," she reasoned. Even after giving birth to three children, Erika found that the longing to adopt still hadn't subsided, so she approached her husband, Barry, with the idea of adding a fourth child to their family. Barry wasn't as certain. Adoption would mean years of paperwork followed by a lot of adjustments to their already full life.

One weekend they attended church as usual, unaware that the guest speaker would be highlighting the great need for families willing to adopt. He talked about God's heart for orphans and encouraged people to open their hearts and homes to give these children a place to grow up surrounded by love. By the time they were in the car on the way home from church, Barry and Erika were on the same page at last, asking God to bring them a child that needed a home.

As a family, they determined that to meet a need, they should go to the place on earth with the greatest need. So they decided on Ethiopia. Ethiopia has a population of about 80 million, and because it has been hit so hard by the AIDS epidemic, there are about 5 million orphans.

Barry and Erika began talking and praying with their children about the little boy they were hoping to adopt. In their conversations they called him Daniel, imagining the little brother who was waiting for them halfway around the world. When they finally received their confirmation letter, their son's picture and a name were included. His Ethiopian name was Hiyab (pronounced HEE-ab), one that none of them had even heard of before. "A lot of kids get renamed when they come home to the United States," Erika said. But when they learned the story behind the name, they immediately knew: "There's no way we can change that!"

Hiyab's birth parents met as teenagers, both of them Ethiopian Orthodox Christians. They moved to the big city of Addis Ababa but split up. They reunited years later, but Hiyab's father died of AIDS before he was born. When she found out she was pregnant and HIV positive, Hiyab's mother did everything she could to educate herself about protecting her baby's health. Because she decided to give birth in a hospital (not the norm in her culture) and take special measures to protect him, her baby was born HIV negative. She named him Hiyab, which means "God's Gift."

Hiyab Daniel is a gift to his family beyond anything they had dreamed of when they prayed and prepared for him. Barry and Erika never imagined what a gift they were giving to their first three children, who adore their little brother. The journey hasn't always been an easy one. During his first week in their home, Hiyab screamed constantly. He was afraid of the dark and had to sleep in Barry and Erika's bed, waking at the smallest sound. He was even afraid of Barry, since his exposure to men had been minimal. But his family's consistent patience and love transformed a scared little boy who spoke no English into a chatty and precocious preschooler who is the light of their lives and often the center of attention in his church and community.

"We plan to take him back to visit Ethiopia one day," Erika says. "We want him to know his story, his heritage. We want him to know where he comes from and the amazing sacrifices his birth mother made so that he can have the life he has today." Knowing where he comes from will be an important part of Hiyab Daniel's life and identity as he grows into the man God is forming him to be.

This week we turn our focus to Daniel. The biblical story of Daniel is one of a young man being raised in a foreign culture, not by loving, adoptive parents, but by a tyrannical government that destroyed his homeland. Daniel moves forward with confidence and integrity in a culture that is foreign to him, but he always maintains the identity of where he came from. His history and homeland, like Hiyab's, will always be a part of him. Daniel never forgot where he came from or the God who went with him no matter where he lived or what name he was called.

Day 1: True to Our Roots

Read God's Word

¹ *In the third year of the reign of Jehoiakim king of Judah, Nebuchadnezzar king of Babylon came to Jerusalem and besieged it.* ² *And the Lord delivered Jehoiakim king of Judah into his hand, along with some of the articles from the temple of God. These he carried off to the temple of his god in Babylonia and put in the treasure house of his god.*

³ *Then the king ordered Ashpenaz, chief of his court officials, to bring in some of the Israelites from the royal family and the nobility—* ⁴ *young men without any physical defect, handsome, showing aptitude for every kind of learning, well informed, quick to understand, and qualified to serve in the king's palace. He was to teach them the language and literature of the Babylonians.* ⁵ *The king assigned them a daily amount of food and wine from the king's table. They were to be trained for three years, and after that they were to enter the king's service.*

⁶ *Among these were some from Judah: Daniel, Hananiah, Mishael and Azariah.* ⁷ *The chief official gave them new names: to Daniel, the name Belteshazzar; to Hananiah, Shadrach; to Mishael, Meshach; and to Azariah, Abednego.*

⁸ *But Daniel resolved not to defile himself with the royal food and wine, and he asked the chief official for permission not to defile himself this way.* ⁹ *Now God had caused the official to show favor and sympathy to Daniel,* ¹⁰ *but the official told Daniel, "I am afraid of my lord the king, who has assigned your food and drink. Why should he see you looking worse than the other young men your age? The king would then have my head because of you."*

¹¹ *Daniel then said to the guard whom the chief official had appointed over Daniel, Hananiah, Mishael and Azariah,* ¹² *"Please test your servants for ten days: Give us nothing but vegetables to eat and water to drink.* ¹³ *Then compare our appearance with that of the young men who eat the royal food, and treat your servants in accordance with what you see."* ¹⁴ *So he agreed to this and tested them for ten days.*

¹⁵ *At the end of the ten days they looked healthier and better nourished than any of the young men who ate the royal food.* ¹⁶ *So the guard took away their choice food and the wine they were to drink and gave them vegetables instead.*

¹⁷ *To these four young men God gave knowledge and understanding of all kinds of literature and learning. And Daniel could understand visions and dreams of all kinds.*

¹⁸ *At the end of the time set by the king to bring them in, the chief official presented them to Nebuchadnezzar.* ¹⁹ *The king talked with them, and he found none equal to Daniel, Hananiah, Mishael and Azariah; so they entered the king's service.* ²⁰ *In every matter of wisdom and understanding about which the king questioned them, he found them ten times better than all the magicians and enchanters in his whole kingdom.*

²¹ *And Daniel remained there until the first year of King Cyrus.*

Daniel 1:1-21

Reflect and Respond

When we're little, our moms seem like know-it-alls. They are the ones in control. They seem to hold all the cards, and they always know what they're doing. Imagine my surprise when I became a mom myself to learn that when they hand you your baby for the first time, they don't hand you the secrets that all moms know, the instructions for what to do at every moment, or the answers to all the questions your children will ask.

On the first night home from the hospital with our first baby, I kicked all the relatives out of the house, imagining our sweet little family of three bonding all alone together. Let's just say that night convinced me of how much I had to learn.

The surprises definitely didn't end in the newborn phase. Lately I'm baffled that I thought parenting one tiny baby was so difficult. Now that he has grown into the toddler trying to run our household, his everyday antics make taking care of his infant sister seem like a piece of cake! Someday I'm sure I will have two teenagers and look back and wonder what all the fuss was about when they were tiny.

Parenting is not for the faint of heart! Running a multimillion-dollar corporation, or a country, is less challenging on some days (not to mention nights) than parenting small children.

Not only do our children start out in the world physically helpless, dependent on us for their needs of nourishment and safety and shelter; they also are a behavioral and social blank slate. They need to be indoctrinated into the family's culture: the expectations of how family members are to treat one another, behave at the table, speak or wait to be called on, and generally function in this particular group of people. We begin teaching our children about the family's culture from the first day they are born. Even newborns receive messages about how structured or chaotic, loud or quiet, loving or distant the family's culture will be. Families teach some of the same lessons, but each of our families is unique in some ways, with its own values, standards, and habits that make it special. Your own family, for example, may have communicated the importance of getting an education, appreciating music or nature, serving the poor, or respecting the wisdom of elders.

Do you have memories of your parents instilling lessons about the behavior and beliefs your family expected of you? Recall one memory and describe it below.

If you're a parent, what are some ways you have instructed your children about your family's culture and beliefs from the beginning?

Train a child in the way he should go, and when he is old he will not turn from it.
Proverbs 22:6

As our children grow, we teach them that our family culture will sometimes differ from those around us: "We don't do that in our family" or "If your friends jumped off a bridge, would you?" Children are absorbing the culture and beliefs of the family around the table at meals, in the car as they are going places, and often just observing our everyday reactions and responses to the world around us.

What does each of these verses say about parenting children who will grow to love God?

Proverbs 22:6 *Start children off on the way they should go, and even when they are old they will not turn from it — Teach them early to love God — manners*

Deuteronomy 11:18-21
Teach your children —
Prayer

Ephesians 6:4
KINDNESS — Teaching — Gods word

2 Timothy 3:16-17
Teaching Gods word
Traing in righteousness

Once upon a time in ancient Jerusalem, four sets of parents began teaching their children what their families believed and what shape their lives were expected to take on the day they were born. They did this by giving them their names. The four boys were named Daniel, Hananiah, Mishael, and Azariah. Their parents knew the first lesson they wanted to teach their sons: that they should honor and worship God in all they did. They felt so strongly about teaching this lesson that they embedded it in their very names. Consider the meanings of their names:

Daniel: God Is My Judge
Hananiah: Yahweh Is Gracious
Mishael: Who Is Like God?
Azariah: Yahweh Has Helped

Each time these boys heard their names, they heard a message about a powerful God who loved and cared for them. The suffix "El" at the end of Daniel's and

Mishael's names can be seen in many of the names of God in Scripture, such as El Shaddai (God Almighty) and El Elyon (Most High God). Other names that include that suffix are Gabriel (Strength of God) and Michael (He Who Is Like God).

In Week 2, Day 5 we learned about the unspoken name of God given to Moses as "I AM" at the burning bush. Although "I AM" in Hebrew is not pronounceable (YHWH has no vowels), it is sometimes pronounced Jehovah or Yahweh when vowels are added. The name Yahweh forms the suffix -aniah or -iah at the end of Hananiah and Azariah's names.

We don't know anything else about Daniel, Hananiah, Mishael, and Azariah's families, but we do know that they made a conscious effort from the first day of their lives to teach them about God and let them know that worshipping the one true God was part of the culture they were born into.

I wonder if those families had a sense of the impending destruction of their surrounding culture and way of life. The Babylonians, under the leadership of King Nebuchadnezzar, invaded and destroyed Jerusalem in 605 B.C., destroying the city and the Temple. The four boys with God-centered names were probably in their early teen years when they became prisoners of war, taken back to the empire of Babylon when their beloved Jerusalem was destroyed.

Reread Daniel 1:3-5.

What were the qualities these young Hebrews possessed that caused the Babylonians to notice them and export them back to their country?

without physical defect, handsome, showing aptitude for every kind of learning, well informed, quick to understand and qualified to serve in the kings palace.

How long was their training period? What would happen to them at the end of it? *3 years — enter the kings service*

Nebuchadnezzar wanted to destroy the culture and convert the people. He wanted to make them Babylonian in culture, education, attitude, and religion. He knew that in order to do that he would need to conquer the hearts and minds of the leaders of the next generation, instilling in them a Babylonian way of life. He did this by taking an entire generation of leaders back to Babylon, where they would be treated not as prisoners of war or as slaves but as trainees for positions of leadership, influence, and power. He knew that if he could convert one generation away from their own religion and way of life, he would reach his goal.

Reread Daniel 1:8-14. What do you notice about the response and attitude of the four young men to the new culture under Daniel's leadership?

Where others saw an opportunity to live a new and lavish lifestyle, Daniel and his friends refused to defile themselves with food and drink that had been offered to Babylonian idols. To eat this food would have meant worshipping those idols. It would have meant a betrayal of their God and all that their parents had instilled in them, starting with their very names.

These young men stood up to the Babylonians, deprived themselves of one incredibly lavish meal after another, and remained true to their names. Their family culture was so embedded in them that even when they were removed from it and transplanted to a pagan environment, their beliefs did not budge. The words of the moms who had been the know-it-alls in their early days still rang in the boys' minds:

If all your friends ate food offered to idols, would you?
Yahweh is gracious (Hananiah)—you can depend on that in the darkest days.
Yahweh has helped (Azariah) us in the past and He will help you through this.
These idols are nothing. There is only one true God. *Who is like Him* (Mishael)?
Don't worry what others say or think or do. Their opinions don't matter.
Only God is your judge (Daniel). Follow His instructions and no others.

That's the kind of strength it takes to hold fast to God's teaching while living in a world where even dinner time is a chance to bow to idols, to give your heart and life to something besides God.

We know all too well that Babylon is not the only culture ever to entice its inhabitants to give their hearts and lives to something besides the one true God.

In what ways does our culture invite us to give our hearts and lives to something besides God?
LIVING IN THE WAYS OF THE WORLD —

How is God's will for our lives different from the typical lifestyle of the culture we live in?

Daniel was a slave & service — a pattern of our thinking
Our attitude was a

How do you handle these differences in your family? How do you instill in your children or grandchildren (or other special children in your life) the ability to live differently than the culture around us?

NOT TO WATCH TV NOT TO LISTEN TO FRIENDS — TALK TO US ABOUT QUESTIONS —

Thank God we are not on our own! We have His Spirit within us to guide us, the power and example of Jesus' life, the teachings of those who have led us to Him to sustain us, and the stories of the faithful, such as Daniel and his friends, to inspire and encourage us. Over the next few days we will see how they remained faithful to their God as the stakes continually got higher and higher.

As you think about how you received your faith through the words and example of faithful Christians before you, I hope you also will notice that the pathway of faith does not stop with you. God has called you to give away your love for Him to those who will come next. How will you pass on this precious treasure?

> The pathway of faith does not stop with you. God has called you to give away your love for Him to those who will come next.

Pray About It

Make three lists as directed below. Pray for each list today and throughout the week.

1. Parents with young children at home. (Pray for patience, energy, physical resources, and an extra measure of love and grace for their children.)

2. Parents with adult children. (Pray for their continued relationship with their adult children and the ways they can be of help to them.)

3. Grandparents you know. (Pray for their influence and relationship with their grandchildren.)

Act on It

- Daniel and his friends were obviously influenced early on by their families, starting with their names. On a separate piece of paper, write a list of beliefs

your family holds. These can be spiritual beliefs or practices or other beliefs your family holds. Read your list to your family members to see if they have things to add. Post your list somewhere in your home.

Day 2: Strangers in a Strange Land

Read God's Word

[8] *At this time some astrologers came forward and denounced the Jews.* [9] *They said to King Nebuchadnezzar, "O king, live forever!* [10] *You have issued a decree, O king, that everyone who hears the sound of the horn, flute, zither, lyre, harp, pipes and all kinds of music must fall down and worship the image of gold,* [11] *and that whoever does not fall down and worship will be thrown into a blazing furnace.* [12] *But there are some Jews whom you have set over the affairs of the province of Babylon—Shadrach, Meshach and Abednego—who pay no attention to you, O king. They neither serve your gods nor worship the image of gold you have set up."*

[13] *Furious with rage, Nebuchadnezzar summoned Shadrach, Meshach and Abednego. So these men were brought before the king,* [14] *and Nebuchadnezzar said to them, "Is it true, Shadrach, Meshach and Abednego, that you do not serve my gods or worship the image of gold I have set up?* [15] *Now when you hear the sound of the horn, flute, zither, lyre, harp, pipes and all kinds of music, if you are ready to fall down and worship the image I made, very good. But if you do not worship it, you will be thrown immediately into a blazing furnace. Then what god will be able to rescue you from my hand?"*

[16] *Shadrach, Meshach and Abednego replied to the king, "O Nebuchadnezzar, we do not need to defend ourselves before you in this matter.* [17] *If we are thrown into the blazing furnace, the God we serve is able to save us from it, and he will rescue us from your hand, O king.* [18] *But even if he does not, we want you to know, O king, that we will not serve your gods or worship the image of gold you have set up."*

[19] *Then Nebuchadnezzar was furious with Shadrach, Meshach and Abednego, and his attitude toward them changed. He ordered the furnace heated seven times hotter than usual* [20] *and commanded some of the strongest soldiers in his army to tie up Shadrach, Meshach and Abednego and throw them into the blazing furnace.* [21] *So these men, wearing their robes, trousers, turbans and other clothes, were bound and thrown into the blazing furnace.* [22] *The king's command was so urgent and the furnace so hot that the flames of the fire killed the soldiers who took up Shadrach, Meshach and Abednego,* [23] *and these three men, firmly tied, fell into the blazing furnace.*

[24] *Then King Nebuchadnezzar leaped to his feet in amazement and asked his advisers, "Weren't there three men that we tied up and threw into the fire?"*

They replied, "Certainly, O king."

[25] *He said, "Look! I see four men walking around in the fire, unbound and unharmed, and the fourth looks like a son of the gods."*

[26] *Nebuchadnezzar then approached the opening of the blazing furnace and shouted, "Shadrach, Meshach and Abednego, servants of the Most High God, come out! Come here!"*

So Shadrach, Meshach and Abednego came out of the fire, [27] *and the satraps, prefects, governors and royal advisers crowded around them. They saw that the fire had not harmed their bodies, nor was a hair of their heads singed; their robes were not scorched, and there was no smell of fire on them.*

[28] *Then Nebuchadnezzar said, "Praise be to the God of Shadrach, Meshach and Abednego, who has sent his angel and rescued his servants! They trusted in him and defied the king's command and were willing to give up their lives rather than serve or worship any god except their own God.* [29] *Therefore I decree that the people of any nation or language who say anything against the God of Shadrach, Meshach and Abednego be cut into pieces and their houses be turned into piles of rubble, for no other god can save in this way."*

[30] *Then the king promoted Shadrach, Meshach and Abednego in the province of Babylon.*

Daniel 3:8-30

Reflect and Respond

When we parted ways after high school graduation, most of us were headed to state colleges a couple of hours from home. But not Allie. She had been dreaming since she was a child of attending an out-of-state college. The idea of starting over where no one had a preconceived notion of her and where she could reinvent herself made her giddy with excitement. She even considered calling herself "Allison" just to make the process of transforming her identity complete.

College life didn't disappoint, and soon Allie had made a group of new friends and was having new adventures. One night just before midterms she was pouring over the study notes for a difficult exam when several girls from her class burst into her dorm room, inviting her to a concert across town. She hesitated and explained that she needed to study, and they ran off to make the next invitation. One girl stayed behind until the others were out of earshot. She told Allie about a secret website where someone had uploaded the answers to the test they were taking the next day. One look and she wouldn't need to study anymore. She could come to the concert with them and be guaranteed a good grade.

Allie didn't even need to consider it. This was part of her identity she didn't want to give up, the one that honored God even when no one was watching. She passed on the concert and the cheating. Though she was rewarded with a lower grade than some others, she received the confirmation that beneath the new surroundings was a part of her that mattered and that had not changed.

Four years later Allie was close to graduating. One of her close friends had just gotten engaged, and some of the girls were treating that friend to a night out to mark the occasion. When dinner was over they all giggled and whispered as they got in the car, heading to their next stop. Allie wasn't quite sure where they were headed. They drove across town and parked in the parking lot of a strip club, where they would continue the bachelorette celebration. They knew Allie well enough by this time to know that she would've found a way to decline if she had known where they were headed. But now she was stuck. Why not come in with them and have some fun? Once again Allie didn't have to think long about her response. Without an ounce of judgment in her voice, she told them she'd just wait in the car until they were ready to go.

Her polite refusal caused each of them to wonder why she wasn't OK with going in and to think a little deeper about why they were. One friend felt bad about her being left in the car and told the others she'd drive Allie back to campus and come back for them later. The friend confided in Allie on the way to the dorm that she had felt uncomfortable too but hadn't had the courage to refuse going along with the crowd. She was impressed that Allie had taken a stand.

Allie was able to grow into a new identity without losing who she really was. She learned that growing up didn't mean growing out of the integrity she had always possessed, both in very private and very public situations.

The four young men in our Bible story were taken from Jerusalem with countless others and transplanted into a strange culture with strange customs and language. The Babylonians wanted to make them feel so at home that they forgot who they were and became completely converted to the language, culture, and religion of Babylon. And one of the first steps toward that end was to change their names.

What new names are given to each of the young men?
Fill in the chart below by reviewing Day 1 and Daniel 1:7 and then reading below.

Old Name	Meaning	New Name
Daniel		
Hananiah		

Old Name	Meaning	New Name
Mishael		
Azariah		

The Babylonians took the names that these young men's parents had given them to honor God and replaced them with names that honored the idols worshipped in Babylon. Some of the changes even deliberately mocked their original names and the God they had been raised to worship. For example, Mishael, which meant "Who Is Like Yahweh?" became Meshach, "Who Is Like Aku?"

The challenges to their integrity and faithfulness to God were immediate upon arrival in Babylon. Not only were they renamed; their first meal called their beliefs into question. In Day 1 we saw that in Babylon they were immediately confronted with the choice of whether or not to eat food sacrificed to idols, a form of idol worship.

We may think, *What's the big deal? It's just a plate of food!* Temptation often starts small. Think of Eve and Adam and a single piece of fruit. No big deal, right? The small temptations toward a white lie, a selfish action, a glance at a website, an unseen act are the most difficult because no one will know but God and us. These young men were able to withstand the temptation to gorge themselves on delicious food because they knew it would betray the God they loved.

Read the following Scriptures. What does each say about what we do in secret, even if no one knows but God and us?

Numbers 32:23

Luke 8:16-17

Matthew 6:6, 18

If eating food that had been on the altar of idols seemed like a small thing, Hananiah, Mishael, and Azariah were given bigger challenges soon enough. They faced a decision about whether to bow down to the ninety-foot-high golden idol statue built by King Nebuchadnezzar. They must have stood out, quite literally, as the crowd around them bowed, and they were the sole people left standing in the presence of the huge idol.

> *But you are a chosen people, a royal priesthood, a holy nation, a people belonging to God...*
> 1 Peter 2:9

Read Exodus 20:4-6. What does God say about bowing to idols?

In the list of the Ten Commandments, which number is this command (see Exodus 20:1-17)?

How is it related to the first commandment?

Standing for God when the rest of the world bows down to things that do not honor Him forces us to call on God for help, to remember who He has called us to be, and to remind ourselves that who we are is not supposed to match up with the crowd around us.

It's OK to stand out. In fact, it's God's intention for His people to be obviously different from everyone else. God created laws for His people that would make it obvious to the world around them that they were different. He expected them to act in ways that were clearly out of synch with the world around them. This was no accident; it was a strategy to make the world take notice. God's people are different because God is different from anything and anyone else.

Look up 1 Peter 2:9 and write the list of phrases used to describe God's people:

1.

2.

3.

In the King James Version, instead of "God's people" or "a people belonging to God," the phrase is translated: "A peculiar people." God's people are special, unique, peculiar. We belong to Him, and He wants it to be obvious to the world. But the world doesn't celebrate peculiarity.

Reread Daniel 3:13-17. What does the king threaten if Hananiah, Mishael, and Azariah do not bow down to the idol, and what is their reply?

Take a look at verses 19 and 20. What orders does the king give in response?

When Hananiah, Mishael, and Azariah made the right decision to stand up to a law that ordered them to worship idols, they weren't rewarded; they were punished. The king's anger burned so greatly that he ordered them to be tied and thrown into a blazing furnace heated seven times hotter than usual, mirroring the combustion of his rage. It's important for us to remember that just because we follow God's will does not mean we're immune to the earthly consequences of our actions, however unfair they may be.

Hananiah, Mishael, and Azariah weren't excused from the fiery furnace just because they did the right thing in God's eyes. The miracle comes, though, when those watching see not three people in the fire, but four.

Reread Daniel 3:25. Who does the king say the fourth figure looks like?

We can't always be sure of our earthly safety because we are God's followers, but we can be sure that God goes with us into the most fiery of situations. When we stand for God, we don't stand alone; He always stands with us.

Read Philippians 2:14-16. How does this passage describe the way we will stand out if we're following God?

Reread Daniel 3:28-30. How does the king's response to the miraculous rescue verify that Hananiah, Mishael, and Azariah were living examples of Philippians 2:14-16?

Whether the act is a private one that no one will know about or a public one that leaves us standing conspicuously while everyone else bows, we all face decisions about whether to go against the tide of the surrounding culture.

How hard is it for you to make God-honoring choices if those choices will make you look or seem "peculiar"?

Our Babylonian transplants faced consequences from small to life threatening and still were able to maintain their identities and honor God. The choices we face may be less dramatic, but God can empower us with equal strength to be peculiarly His and stand up for Him in a world that bows down.

Pray About It

How are you being called to stand up and honor God when others are bowing down to the idols that our culture honors? Ask God to give you the courage and strength to take a stand. And pray for others you know who are being called to take a stand as well.

Act on It

- While the decisions we face to go against the flow and do God's will seem big to us, they pale in comparison to Christians who live in lands where their faith could result in persecution or even death. Learn more about the persecuted church by visiting the Voice of the Martyrs website (www. persecution.com). What action can you take to help the persecuted church around the world?

Day 3: Worship: The Soul's Oxygen

Read God's Word

[1] *It pleased Darius to appoint 120 satraps to rule throughout the kingdom,*
[2] *with three administrators over them, one of whom was Daniel. The satraps were*

made accountable to them so that the king might not suffer loss. ³ Now Daniel so distinguished himself among the administrators and the satraps by his exceptional qualities that the king planned to set him over the whole kingdom. ⁴ At this, the administrators and the satraps tried to find grounds for charges against Daniel in his conduct of government affairs, but they were unable to do so. They could find no corruption in him, because he was trustworthy and neither corrupt nor negligent. ⁵ Finally these men said, "We will never find any basis for charges against this man Daniel unless it has something to do with the law of his God."

⁶ So the administrators and the satraps went as a group to the king and said: "O King Darius, live forever! ⁷ The royal administrators, prefects, satraps, advisers and governors have all agreed that the king should issue an edict and enforce the decree that anyone who prays to any god or man during the next thirty days, except to you, O king, shall be thrown into the lions' den. ⁸ Now, O king, issue the decree and put it in writing so that it cannot be altered—in accordance with the laws of the Medes and Persians, which cannot be repealed." ⁹ So King Darius put the decree in writing.

¹⁰ Now when Daniel learned that the decree had been published, he went home to his upstairs room where the windows opened toward Jerusalem. Three times a day he got down on his knees and prayed, giving thanks to his God, just as he had done before. ¹¹ Then these men went as a group and found Daniel praying and asking God for help. ¹² So they went to the king and spoke to him about his royal decree: "Did you not publish a decree that during the next thirty days anyone who prays to any god or man except to you, O king, would be thrown into the lions' den?"

The king answered, "The decree stands—in accordance with the laws of the Medes and Persians, which cannot be repealed."

¹³ Then they said to the king, "Daniel, who is one of the exiles from Judah, pays no attention to you, O king, or to the decree you put in writing. He still prays three times a day." ¹⁴ When the king heard this, he was greatly distressed; he was determined to rescue Daniel and made every effort until sundown to save him.

¹⁵ Then the men went as a group to the king and said to him, "Remember, O king, that according to the law of the Medes and Persians no decree or edict that the king issues can be changed."

¹⁶ So the king gave the order, and they brought Daniel and threw him into the lions' den. The king said to Daniel, "May your God, whom you serve continually, rescue you!"

Daniel 6:1-16

Reflect and Respond

I once worked as a youth minister in a small church where the church secretary was over ninety years old. Her vision was spotty, and so her typing was, in a word, entertaining. The teenagers in our church used to make a game when they lost interest in the sermons by circling the typos in the church bulletin. Although our secretary was unique to say the least, it turns out we weren't the only church that was titillated by typos.

Besides providing hymn numbers and liturgy, church bulletins often provide entertainment for those in the pews. Here are a couple that have actually appeared in church bulletins:

This evening at 7 PM there will be a hymn sing in the park across from the church. Bring a blanket and come prepared to sin.
Remember in prayer the many that are sick of our community.

One little letter can change singers to sinners. One misplaced word makes people sick in the church sick *of* the church. Who says you can't laugh in church? There's one particular church bulletin typo that is my favorite, although not because it makes people giggle. I like to look for it because I believe it's by far the most common. By my estimates, this word is probably misspelled half the time in church bulletins. See if you can detect it.

During Communion, those who feel led may come forward for prayer at the alter.

Did you catch it? We see the word *alter* so often that it seems appropriate to substitute it for *altar*, usually the word we mean to use in church. Only one letter is different, yet this one letter completely changes the meaning.

Alter: To make different, to change or modify, to cause a transformation

Altar: A structure, typically a table, at which religious rites are performed. The central structure in Christian worship and Holy Communion.

The reason this one little misspelling appeals to me is that I think *alter* is an appropriate word for what happens to us during worship. Worship changes us. It alters us. When we gather around an altar as a community of believers, something in our hearts is transformed, modified, made different. Worship can transform our situation and surroundings until we find ourselves no longer in a dark sanctuary but at the throne of God. Worship shifts our focus outside ourselves and reminds us that there is a greater reality beyond the struggles we face.

Read the following verses. For each, write a word or phrase describing a characteristic or result of worship.

Psalm 34:8

Psalm 95:6

James 4:8

Philippians 2:9-11

Revelation 5:11-14

When Daniel worshipped, it took him beyond the borders of Babylon and back to the Temple in Jerusalem where he had worshipped as a boy. As he worshipped and prayed to God, Daniel was no longer a prisoner in a foreign land; he was a citizen of the kingdom of God.

So, when a decree from the king said that no one could worship or pray to anyone but the king for a full month, Daniel was put in a tough situation. His three friends had faced a law that attempted to force them to worship something false. Now he was faced with a law that tried to force him *not* to worship something true. This law was orchestrated by his enemies, who were deliberately trying to trap him.

Reread Daniel 6:10. What did Daniel do when he heard the decree?

How many times a day does it say that Daniel prayed?

The fact that Daniel prayed three times every day in the same place, facing the direction of Jerusalem, was well known; and it tells us a lot about him. We know that he was faithful to worship God even in this foreign land where he was surrounded by a false religion. How easy it would have been to believe God was far away, unfeeling, or uncaring. Yet Daniel turned to God in prayer faithfully.

According to Daniel 6:10, what did Daniel do during his prayer time?

NAMESAKE

Our need to
worship God does
not change with
our shifting
circumstances.

When we are struggling with harsh realities or simply the monotony of daily life, praising God is often not at the top of our list of things we feel like doing. But our need to worship God does not change with our shifting circumstances. Daniel made worship a habit. If we will do the same, we will find that praise grounds us in a reality beyond our moods or our situations. Worship gives deep gladness to the heart of God. It also grounds us in a reality that is unseen—one that is more true than those before our eyes.

How does offering praise and worship affect or change you?

Daniel found a place to worship even when it wasn't convenient or safe. He prayed to God when he may have felt very distant from God. This daily practice of prayer and worship helped Daniel and his friends keep their faith strong when faced with tough choices. Daniel's prayer life and his ability to stay true to God, continuing to worship even when it meant his life was at stake, are intrinsically connected. His continual seeking of God's heart through worship helped him do what was right even when the stakes were high.

Reread Daniel 6:11-16. What was the consequence of Daniel's decision to disobey the king's decree?

Don't miss this: *Worship prepared Daniel to face the lions' den.*

God knew that worship would be as important to us as the air we breathe. When we're living in an atmosphere that could choke the faith out of us, making worship a priority is as important as taking oxygen on a deep-sea diving expedition.

The emphasis on worship is found throughout Scripture. The Psalms are packed with praise and worship to God. Revelation shines with Technicolor images of worship before the lamb on the throne. The book of Exodus dedicates thirteen chapters to instructions about the building of the Tabernacle, a traveling center of worship for God's people. The attention given to worship in so many situations in the Bible shows us how important worship is to God.

What do you discover about the importance of worship in these different situations in Scripture?

Exodus 25:8-9

Psalm 100

Revelation 4:8-11

Solitary prayer, like Daniel practiced from the window that faced Jerusalem in his room each day, is an important part of the Christian life. As important as it is to pray alone, it is also vital to our spiritual health to gather and worship together. Getting together with brothers and sisters of faith makes our individual voices of praise, confession, and petition one strong common voice lifted to God. Worshipping together helps keep us from wandering off on our own diversions, bonds us with other believers, and reminds us that we are never alone.

Daniel, Hananiah, Mishael, and Azariah had the benefit of being together in exile. While they didn't have their families or their homeland, they had each other, a fact that likely helped sustain them and guide them in the tough choices they were forced to make.

When has a community of faith sustained you through a difficult time in your own life?

There are stories from many other wars in history that show how faith and solidarity sustained men and women like Daniel and his friends after they had been captured by the enemy—stories of prisoners of war passing Bibles back and forth and whispering verses and hymns through cell walls. These acts, though small, gave them hope. Although we aren't imprisoned, we do live in a land that is not our home. Knowing that we are not alone in our faith has an amazing effect of helping us stay spiritually alive in the most difficult of times.

Worship is the redirection of our hearts to the heart of God. It's the corporate gathering of God's people into one family. It's the pure oxygen we need to breathe to keep our faith alive! Find a time this week that you can gather with other believers, direct your attention and worship to God, and breathe deeply.

> Worship is the redirection of our hearts to the heart of God.

127

Pray About It

Daniel prayed from a window that faced Jerusalem, his homeland, something close to his heart. Find a "window" for your prayer time today. Choose a picture, a cross, or something else you can use to visualize and focus your prayer. If you are praying for a specific person or need, write or draw something in the space below that symbolizes the need. Pray with your eyes open, letting God direct your prayers through the window you have chosen.

Act on It

- Shake up your practices of prayer and worship this week. Find new places and ways to pray. Notice any changes in your attitude or situation.

Day 4: Beasts of Burden

[1] *Bel bows down, Nebo stoops low; their idols are borne by beasts of burden.*
The images that are carried about are burdensome,
 a burden for the weary.
[2] *They stoop and bow down together;*
 unable to rescue the burden,
 they themselves go off into captivity.
 [3] *"Listen to me, O house of Jacob,*
 all you who remain of the house of Israel,
you whom I have upheld since you were conceived,
 and have carried since your birth.
[4] *Even to your old age and gray hairs*
 I am he, I am he who will sustain you.
I have made you and I will carry you;
 I will sustain you and I will rescue you.
 [5] *"To whom will you compare me or count me equal?*
 To whom will you liken me that we may be compared?
[6] *Some pour out gold from their bags*

and weigh out silver on the scales;
they hire a goldsmith to make it into a god,
and they bow down and worship it.
⁷ They lift it to their shoulders and carry it;
they set it up in its place, and there it stands.
From that spot it cannot move.
Though one cries out to it, it does not answer;
it cannot save him from his troubles.
⁸ "Remember this, fix it in mind,
take it to heart, you rebels.
⁹ Remember the former things, those of long ago;
I am God, and there is no other;
I am God, and there is none like me.

Isaiah 46:1-9

Reflect and Respond

I love to read. You might even say that books are a bit of an addiction for me. The evidence is obvious: my home and office are overflowing with bookshelves, which are overflowing with books. I even got engaged in a bookstore!

So when one of my favorite authors (and one of my heroes in faith), Ellsworth Kalas, announced in a seminary class that he was about to tell us the three most important books we could ever read in life, I sat up straight and took notice. My pen was poised and ready to scribble down authors' names and titles. Surely the first one would be the Bible. But what after that? I was sure my life was about to be changed by his choices. It certainly was.

"The three most important books you'll ever read in life," Dr. Kalas announced, "are your checkbook, your datebook, and your diary."

I remember my initial confusion. Then Dr. Kalas went on to tell us that these three "books" could teach us more about our hearts than any other book we could read. They teach us where we spend our money, our time, and our attention. If we understand these three things about ourselves, we have a starting point to know what holds the place of utmost importance in our lives, what we worship.

Worship is far more than what happens in an hour-long church service on Sunday morning. It's about letting something become our reason for living and purpose in life.

Human beings are innately created to worship. It's part of our makeup as spiritual beings. We all assign the role of god to something. To find out what that might be, we only have to follow the paper trail left in our checkbooks, calendars, and journals. If we track the decisions and motivations recorded in

We all assign the role of god to something. To find out what that might be, we only have to follow the paper trail left in our checkbooks, calendars, and journals.

those three books, we'll discover what we truly value. Worship is more than just belief. It means orienting our lives to give honor to something beyond ourselves. Whatever we put at the center of our lives is what we worship.

Worshipping an invisible God takes quite a leap of faith. It's so much easier to believe in what we can see and touch with our hands than in a God we cannot see. To fix this problem, the Babylonians (and many other cultures like them) made idols, physical statues or representations of their gods. These were made of wood or metal and placed on an altar where people could worship them, bow to them, and make sacrifices to them.

What do these verses teach us about making idols and worshipping false gods?

Psalm 115:4-8

Romans 1:21-23

1 Corinthians 10:21

Matthew 4:8-10

As we've seen, the leaders of Babylon tried to force Daniel, Hananiah, Mishael, and Azariah to take God from the center of their lives and put false gods and idols in His place. Since God held a place of honor in their names, the Babylonian leaders took away those names and replaced them with names honoring false gods, idols. The gods at the center of their new names were Bel, Aku, and Nebo.

Daniel became Belteshazzar. Bel signifies the title "Lord" or "Master" rather than a proper name. This title was possibly used to signify Marduk, one of many Babylonian gods. Hananiah and Mishael became Shadrach and Meshach, with the idol Aku at the heart of their new names, the Babylonian god of wisdom. Azariah became Abednego, to honor Nebo, the Babylonian god of the moon.

The Bible addresses the damaging nature of idol worship in a poetic chapter of Isaiah. It actually brings up some of the exact idols mentioned in the new names Daniel and his friends received.

Bel bows down, Nebo stoops low;
 their idols are borne by beasts of burden.
The images that are carried about are burdensome,
 a burden for the weary.
They stoop and bow down together;
 unable to rescue the burden,
 they themselves go off into captivity.
                                        Isaiah 46:1-2

The imagery of these first two verses is of large, heavy idols placed on the backs of donkeys or oxen to be moved. Instead of powerfully lifting burdens, these idols themselves become a burden. Instead of freeing people from captivity, they themselves can be carried into captivity.

God's objection to people worshipping false idols is less about His need for adoration and more about how horribly it affects our lives when we give our worship away to the wrong things. God insists that we worship Him not because He is self-interested but because abiding in His character is in the best interest of His children.

Take a moment to go back and circle every word in Isaiah 46:1-2 that supports the imagery of lowering, burdening, or stooping down. How many words did you circle?

God cares about us so much that He wants us to orient our lives to worship the only thing that can unburden us, Him! God mourns the fact that while people should be bowing to the God who made them and can save them, instead they are carrying around heavy idols. In the images of Isaiah 46, God ridicules the idols for themselves bowing down because they are causing such a burden to the people and animals forced to carry them.

Instead of lifting people's burdens, these idols cause an extra burden on their lives, adding to the burdens they were hoping the idols would help to alleviate. The truth is that idol worship damages our lives. It's a tragic irony that the very idols we suppose will save us are the things that destroy us.

God loves us so fiercely that He fights to destroy anything that could harm us. It's no accident that when God hands out the Ten Commandments for His people to follow, He begins with these two:

> "I am the LORD your God, who brought you out of Egypt, out of the land of slavery.
> "You shall have no other gods before me.
> "You shall not make for yourself an idol in the form of anything in heaven above or on the earth beneath or in the waters below. You shall not bow down to them or worship them; for I, the LORD your God, am a jealous God, punishing the children for the sin of the fathers to the third and fourth generation of those who hate me, but showing love to a thousand generations of those who love me and keep my commandments."
>
> Exodus 20:2-6

Why do you think God gave these first two commandments?

Why do you think He began by reminding the people of their history as slaves in Egypt?

> Idols will always burden us. God will always lift our burdens.

Exodus 20 reminds us that only God can save, that He brought His people out of Egypt, where they were slaves. This reminder is closely connected to the command that they should have no other gods and should not make idols. The implication is that when we turn to anything but God for help, we are deceiving ourselves, burdening ourselves, and separating ourselves from the help and salvation He is so eager to give. The benefits of choosing to worship God impact not only our own lives but also trickle down to thousands of generations that will follow.

While our current culture doesn't often create physical idols to represent false gods (statues of clay and wood and bronze), we do have a problem with idol worship. We adopt things in our own lives and place them in the seat that God alone should occupy. We may take relationships or control, worry or financial resources, jobs or children, desires for food or sex, beauty or wealth, and begin to make them the center of our thoughts and priorities.

The question at the heart of the book of Daniel is this: *What will you worship?*

Daniel and his three friends are given that choice again and again. Will you eat food offered to idols? Will you bow down to a golden statue? Will you pray to the king instead of praying daily to the God you love? Each conflict they face, each major choice they make, is about choosing whom they will worship.

The same is true for us. The most basic conflicts of our lives arise when we begin to worship things besides God. When we turn our lives over to Him, our most basic records (like our checkbook, calendar, and journal) will indicate choices that honor Him, decisions we've made because we want to be more like Him. His name and His character will shine through the line items, daily entries, and appointments, and our lives will reflect His joy because of it.

Idols will always burden us. God will always lift our burdens.

What are the idols we commonly worship in our culture—things that draw our attention, money, and passion in a way that diminishes our love for God?

What are things in your own life that attract you to pay greater attention to them than to God?

An awareness of the ways our hearts easily slip into the worship of other things is the first step in turning them back to God. When we remind ourselves again that He is the source of our comfort and strength, the giver of every good and perfect gift, the choice to worship Him with our whole lives flows naturally. I hope that you have discovered the joy of worshipping the One who unburdens, who lifts up, who brings peace and contentment. In a world filled with competitors for our attention, He is the one choice as object of our affection who will give more love than He could ever receive.

Pray About It

God, forgive us for worshipping things other than You. Help us to recognize what it is we bow down to and how much it burdens us. Then turn our attention, respect, love, and worship fully to You. Unburden us. Free us. Help us to place You at the center of our lives. Amen.

Act on It

- Set aside time to discover the idols that might be revealed in your three most important books. Sit down with these three in front of you:

  1. Your checkbook (or debit card statement)
  2. Your datebook/calendar (or electronic device with your e-calendar)
  3. Your diary or journal, or any notes you've made over the last year about events or activities in your life

  As you flip through these three revealing resources, make some notes here about how you spend your money, your time, and your thoughts. Do you notice any trends? What do these books reveal about what is most important to you? Have any of these become idols to you?

People / Victims of the (enemy) —

Day 5: Revelation—Integrity in a Name

Read God's Word

²⁶ *Nebuchadnezzar then approached the opening of the blazing furnace and shouted, "Shadrach, Meshach and Abednego, servants of the Most High God, come out! Come here!"*

So Shadrach, Meshach and Abednego came out of the fire, ²⁷ *and the satraps, prefects, governors and royal advisers crowded around them. They saw that the fire had not harmed their bodies, nor was a hair of their heads singed; their robes were not scorched, and there was no smell of fire on them.*

²⁸ *Then Nebuchadnezzar said, "Praise be to the God of Shadrach, Meshach and Abednego, who has sent his angel and rescued his servants! They trusted in him and defied the king's command and were willing to give up their lives rather than serve or worship any god except their own God.* ²⁹ *Therefore I decree that the people of any nation or language who say anything against the God of Shadrach, Meshach and Abednego be cut into pieces and their houses be turned into piles of rubble, for no other god can save in this way."*

³⁰ *Then the king promoted Shadrach, Meshach and Abednego in the province of Babylon.*

Daniel 3:26-30

¹⁷ *A stone was brought and placed over the mouth of the den, and the king sealed it with his own signet ring and with the rings of his nobles, so that Daniel's situation might not be changed.* ¹⁸ *Then the king returned to his palace and spent the night without eating and without any entertainment being brought to him. And he could not sleep.*

¹⁹ *At the first light of dawn, the king got up and hurried to the lions' den.* ²⁰ *When he came near the den, he called to Daniel in an anguished voice, "Daniel, servant of the living God, has your God, whom you serve continually, been able to rescue you from the lions?"*

²¹ *Daniel answered, "O king, live forever!* ²² *My God sent his angel, and he shut the mouths of the lions. They have not hurt me, because I was found innocent in his sight. Nor have I ever done any wrong before you, O king."*

²³ *The king was overjoyed and gave orders to lift Daniel out of the den. And when Daniel was lifted from the den, no wound was found on him, because he had trusted in his God.*

²⁴ *At the king's command, the men who had falsely accused Daniel were brought in*

and thrown into the lions' den, along with their wives and children. And before they reached the floor of the den, the lions overpowered them and crushed all their bones.

²⁵ Then King Darius wrote to all the peoples, nations and men of every language throughout the land:

"May you prosper greatly!

²⁶ "I issue a decree that in every part of my kingdom people must fear and reverence the God of Daniel.

"For he is the living God
and he endures forever;
his kingdom will not be destroyed,
his dominion will never end.
²⁷ He rescues and he saves;
he performs signs and wonders
in the heavens and on the earth.
He has rescued Daniel
from the power of the lions."

²⁸ So Daniel prospered during the reign of Darius and the reign of Cyrus the Persian.

Daniel 6:17-28

Reflect and Respond

A commercial flashes across the TV screen. A shiny new product is center stage. A gorgeous celebrity enters. We recognize her as beautiful, talented, sexy, and cool. She picks up the product and flashes a winning smile at the camera. We get the message: use this product and you will be just like me.

In our consumer-driven culture, celebrity endorsements of products are commonplace. Companies look for celebrities to use their products, do their commercials, and wear their logos. Celebrities lend their "name" to products so that their image becomes the face of the brand. It's a match made in a lawyer's office, with stacks of contracts creating what everyone hopes will be a win-win situation for all the parties involved.

Besides detailing the commercials to be shot and the money to be exchanged, huge portions of those contracts have to do with the conduct of the celebrities while they're serving as the face of the company. There are certain behaviors they must avoid, places they must not be photographed, words they are not allowed to say. Their behavior will reflect on the product they endorse, so the company gets to tell them what kinds of things they can and cannot do in order to preserve the integrity of the product's image. Some sports celebrities have been through

135

periods of scandal where they lost endorsement deals because companies no longer found them worthy to wear their name.

When we enter into relationship with God, we are given the incredible privilege of wearing His name. We become the face of God to the people we meet, His representatives on earth. This is both an awesome mark of favor and a sobering responsibility.

What do these verses teach us about being God's representatives?

2 Corinthians 5:18-21

Colossians 3:15-17

1 Corinthians 3:16-17

Moses' encounter with God at the burning bush led him to ask God: "Suppose I go to the Israelites and say to them 'The God of your fathers has sent me to you,' and they ask me, 'What is his name?' Then what shall I tell them?" (Exodus 3:13).

Moses was looking for an endorsement, a name, a base of credibility that He could carry back with Him to God's people. God endorsed the purpose and ministry He had given Moses by giving Him a name: "I AM who I AM. This is what you are to say to the Israelites: 'I AM has sent me to you'" (Exodus 3:14). Any brilliant leadership decision Moses made, any miracle he performed, wasn't in his own strength or his own name but in the name of YHWH, the "I AM." Everything Moses did was an endorsement of God's name and power.

The same is true in the story of Daniel and his friends. The famous account of Hananiah, Mishael, and Azariah, which we studied on Day 2, ends with them walking out of the fiery furnace without a mark on them, unsinged and unharmed. King Nebuchadnezzar, who had ordered them burned to death, was impressed, to say the least, but he wasn't impressed with *them*; he clearly saw that their actions pointed beyond them to the God they represented.

Reread Daniel 3:28-29. What is the king's reaction? What does he say?

Remember that this is the same king who had a golden statue of himself built and demanded people bow down to it. What factors do you think brought about this change in him?

A similar change occurred in another king of Babylon some years later. On Day 3 we read about Daniel defying King Darius's decree that no one could pray to any god or man except him, and we saw that he was sentenced to be thrown into a den of lions. Today we pick up the story where we left off.

Reread Daniel 6:17-23.

What do they do to ensure that Daniel cannot escape the lions' den?

What does King Darius find when he rushes to the lions' den the next morning?

Who does Daniel say shut the mouths of the lions?

When Daniel survived a night in the lions' den, King Darius changed his tune completely. Instead of demanding that all people pray only to the king, he issued another decree.

Reread Daniel 6:26-27.

What does the king discover about God?

What does he decree that people must do?

Remember that this is the same king who issued a decree demanding that people pray only to him. What do you think caused his change of heart?

In Week 2 of our study, we learned about the integrity at the heart of God.

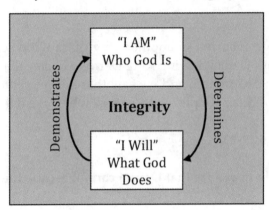

Who God is and what God does are in perfect harmony. God's character determines what He does, and what He does demonstrates His character to the world. We never have to second-guess God because we know He will always act based on the goodness at His core. There is integrity—consistency—between who God is and what God does.

A similar thing can be said of us. Regardless of what kind of character we have, who we are on the inside inevitably determines our actions, and our actions demonstrate what kind of character we have.

Read Luke 6:43-45 and fill in the blanks.

"A good tree doesn't produce bad fruit, nor does a bad tree produce good fruit. Each tree is known by its ___own___ ___fruit___. People don't gather figs from thorny plants, nor do they pick grapes from prickly bushes. A ___good___ person produces ___good___ from the good treasury of the inner self, while an ___inner___ person produces ___inner___ from the evil treasury of the inner self. The inner self overflows with words that are spoken." **(CEB)**

I don't know about you, but when I begin to search deeply into the contents of my heart, I'm not always proud of what I find there. The more closely I look at my own motivations, the more I know that I need God to continue His transforming work in me. If I don't turn those dark places over to Him, I know they will come to light in my actions and relationships.

The good news is that God isn't done with me—or with you! He continues to work in our hearts throughout our lives in a process of change called *sanctification*, which is transformation. This transforming action means that we can grow to reflect God's character.

> [God] continues to work in our hearts throughout our lives in a process of change called *sanctification*, which is transformation.

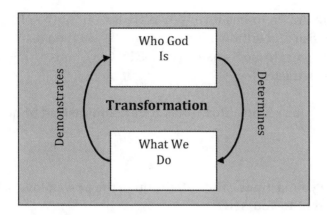

When we let God transform us, when we wear His name at the core of our being, who God is begins to determine our actions. The closer we get to Him, the more our actions and relationships reflect His character. On the other side of this circle of transformation, we find that when our lives begin to show the changes God is making in our hearts, other people notice. If we are true to the God whose nature is determining our actions, people will not look *at* us but *through* us to the God behind our transformation.

Read Matthew 5:14-16. Who will people praise when they see our good deeds?

Notice that it doesn't say people will see our good deeds and praise *us*. It says that they will see our good deeds and praise our Father. When we allow God to transform us, what we do bears witness to God's character, witnessing to the work He is doing in us and drawing others to Him.

That is exactly what happened in the lives of Daniel, Hananiah, Mishael, and Azariah. The character of these men pointed people to honor God, not them. It's amazing to read about the murderous, idolatrous kings of Babylon changing their tune and worshipping God when they saw Him at work in Daniel's and his friends' lives. Even though in these particular instances Daniel and his friends were promoted and their own lives benefitted, the true outcome of their actions was to build up God's name, not their own.

Psalm 23:3 says: "He leads me in paths of righteousness for his name's sake" (ESV). When we walk in paths of righteousness, when we act and treat others in ways that reflect God's character, it's His name, not our own, that is lifted up. This is the exact opposite of the actions at the Tower of Babel, where people were working to make a name for themselves. When we allow God to transform us, we act in order to call attention to God; we live for His name's sake, not our own.

It's sobering to think that our own actions affect God's credibility—that, like celebrities endorsing a product, people see us as "the face" of the faith we pro- claim. When we live the way Christ lived, people see His nature reflected in our

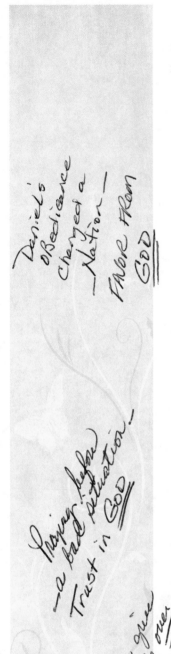

actions and are drawn to His love. When we act out of the places in our hearts that are still selfish and untransformed, *we* are the ones on display for the world. The greatest damage to God's name is done by Christians acting in ways that do not reflect His character.

When have your actions hurt God's reputation instead of helping it?

When have your actions called attention to the power, love, and character of God instead of to yourself?

God calls us to live so differently from the people around us that they take notice. He calls us to live the way Jesus did. Daniel, Hananiah, Mishael, and Azariah had God's name embedded in their own names. When we make a pledge to follow Jesus, He gives us the name "Christian" to wear—a title that has the very name of Christ embedded in it. If we allow Him to continually transform our hearts and actions, we will bring honor and praise not to ourselves but to Christ, for His name's sake.

Pray About It

Unchanging God, help us to change so that we may reflect Your love and compassion. If there are parts of our lives that are not in step with the name of Christ, which we are given the privilege of wearing, help us to recognize them and turn them over to You. We praise You for the ways You have been at work, making us like Jesus. We still need Your help! Make us over into Your image so that people will see You in us and praise Your name. Lead us in paths of righteousness, not for our sake, but for the sake of Your name. Amen.

Act on It

- Think of your life as a commercial for God's loving, transforming action. How are you doing at endorsing the product of His grace? Would people want to buy the product based on the way you treat them? Based on your actions and relationships? If there is a part of your life that does not reflect integrity or consistency with the name of Christ, how can you work on it this week?

Week 4
VIDEO VIEWER GUIDE

Copying the culture around us means that we _Blend_ into our surrounding culture so well that no one notices anything _Different_ about us.

Condemning the culture around us means looking with _secular_ on everything that is _____, separating ourselves from everything outside of things in the Christian church.

Idol: An image of a ~~false~~ _God_, calling you to worship that image itself

Icon: A visible image that points you to worship an _invisible_ _____

Now when Daniel learned that the decree had been published, he went home to his upstairs room where the windows opened toward _Jerusalem_. *Three times a day he got down on his knees and* _prayed_, *giving thanks to his God, just as he had done before.*

Daniel 6:10 NIV

Mostly our _Culture_ calls us to worship _ourselves_.

If you want to resist the cultural temptation to make yourself a _god_ . . . just become an _icon_. Tell people, "Don't look at me. Look _through_ me . . . to the God I worship."

Daniel —
GOD is my Judge

LIVE and BE DIFFERENT

141

Week 5
Peter
Every Name Tells a Story: Pedro

When I arrived at the hospital having contractions at the end of my second pregnancy, I was very excited when the doctor told me that, yes, this was really labor and, yes, I would be having a baby girl today. My second favorite news of the morning was when the doctor told me that I could get my epidural. My contractions were in full force, and the epidural is my favorite part of having a baby (I'm not joking). Seeing new life come into the world is great, but the epidural. . . . Whoever invented it is definitely the greatest inventor who ever lived—next to the person who discovered chocolate.

For some reason, the sweet anesthesiologist thought it would be a good idea for Jim to stay in the room, sit on a stool facing me, and hold my hand while I got the epidural—you know, to comfort me. Here are some facts that might have changed that decision. Fact one: I have a medical background and a great fondness for the epidural (previously mentioned), and I was not in the slightest need of comfort. Fact two: That is one huge needle going into your spine. Fact three: Jim has sometimes been known to pass out when giving blood, something that requires a much smaller needle and a situation with nowhere near as much stress and excitement.

So, as the nice doctor was placing a needle into a place inches away from where it could cause paralysis, I stared into my husband's eyes as his face turned white, his eyes rolled back in his head, the stool rolled out from under him, and his head made a loud knocking sound while connecting with the hospital floor. All the while the nice doctor with the needle in my back was screaming in my ear: "Do not move! Do not move!" (Note: If you ever meet my husband, please don't mock him. He was kind enough to give permission for me to write about this!)

Suddenly the entire emergency response team was in the room with us, and I wasn't the patient everyone was most concerned about. Jim regained consciousness immediately, but the medical staff insisted that he make a trip to the emergency room for a CAT scan. I agreed we were better safe than sorry, so off he went to give our hospital bills a creative addendum.

In the meantime, our medical team was focused on helping me *not* to deliver a baby while my husband was away in another part of the hospital. My labor was progressing, and I was worried that Jim would miss the delivery, something we never imagined would happen. My blood pressure was going up for several reasons, and the staff was trying to calm me down and reassure me that Jim would be fine.

The anesthesiologist tried to distract me. "Let me tell you a funny story," he said. "Once I was delivering a baby for a woman who spoke very little English. She was a pretty tough-looking lady, but she seemed a bit scared, so I had the father stay in the room during the epidural. He did the same thing your husband did! He passed out cold—head hit the floor. We were all trying to rouse him. I was standing behind this woman, and she had a huge tattoo with the name 'Jose' in large letters covering her back. So I began to yell at the man on the floor: 'Jose! Jose! Wake up!' He opened his eyes and gave me a very strange look, and the pregnant woman looked over her shoulder and very coldly said: 'His name is Pedro.' I guess that tattoo wasn't for him after all!"

His story worked. I laughed out loud. Jim returned soon after with a clean bill of health, and our little Kate was born without much delay. We were so grateful for a positive outcome, an amazing hospital staff, and the safe arrival of our baby girl. If she had been a boy, we might have had to consider the name Pedro just to remember the strange happenings of that day!

Our biblical story this week is one with plenty of unexpected twists. Simon Peter was a man no one would have predicted would become a follower of the living God, much less a leader of the church. He was rough around the edges to say the least, but Jesus saw in him something that God could use. Peter's story is so encouraging to those of us who need our rough edges sanded off by God's grace. He reminds us that God is not only a builder of great creations; He also specializes in renovating and rebuilding. No one was more aware of or more grateful for that fact than Peter. And just to make you smile, don't forget that if you say it in Spanish, his name is Pedro!

Day 1: From Mess to Ministry

Read God's Word

¹³ When Jesus came to the region of Caesarea Philippi, he asked his disciples, "Who do people say the Son of Man is?"

¹⁴ They replied, "Some say John the Baptist; others say Elijah; and still others, Jeremiah or one of the prophets."

¹⁵ "But what about you?" he asked. "Who do you say I am?"

¹⁶ Simon Peter answered, "You are the Christ, the Son of the living God."

¹⁷ Jesus replied, "Blessed are you, Simon son of Jonah, for this was not revealed to you by man, but by my Father in heaven. ¹⁸ And I tell you that you are Peter, and on this rock I will build my church, and the gates of Hades will not overcome it."

Matthew 16:13-18

Reflect and Respond

When I answered the call to follow Jesus, I was a mess—selfish and immature. As it became clear to me that God loved me and wanted a better life for me, I often had doubts that I was worthy of God's love. I wasn't sure why He would choose me to be His follower, much less a leader.

I remember thinking that the people in the Bible were perfect, holy examples for us to follow—examples I knew I'd never live up to. After all, why did we call them "Saint Matthew" or "Saint John" on our church signs? When I got to the story of Simon, however, there was no denying that this guy was no saint! I remember reading about Simon Peter's antics, trying hard to figure out why this perfectly flawed person had been given such a central place in Jesus' perfect story. It helped me to figure out that while he wasn't a saint, he was an ordinary man that I could identify with. If God loved Simon Peter and thought He could use him for good, there might just be hope for me as well!

When Simon answered the call to follow Jesus, he was a mess. He was impulsive, brash, immature, and reckless. His temper flared and he usually spoke up before his brain could intervene. Jesus knew He had His work cut out for Him where Simon was concerned. But for some reason, Jesus chose Simon. Not only was he chosen to be a follower; he was chosen as a leader for the disciples and the ragtag collection of imperfect people who would come to be called the church.

How do we know that Jesus singled out Simon Peter as a leader?

Four times in the New Testament the disciples are listed, as if in a roll call, in Matthew, Mark, Luke, and Acts. The order in which they are named varies slightly. But each time they are listed in an order that basically can be divided into three groups of four.

Look up the four passages in which the disciples are named. Write the disciples' names in the exact order that they are mentioned each time.

Matthew 10:2-4	Mark 3:16-19	Luke 6:13-16	Acts 1:13-14
1. Simon/Peter	1. Simon/Peter	1. Simon/Peter	1. Peter
2. Andrew	2. James/Zeb	2. Andrew	2. John
3. James/Zeb	3. John	3. James	3. James
4. John	4. Andrew	4. John	4. Andrew
5. Phillip	5. Phillip	5. Phillip	5. Phillip
6. Bartholomew	6. Bartholomew	6. Bartholomew	6. Thomas
7. Thomas	7. Matthew	7. Matthew	7. Bartholomew
8. Matthew	8. Thomas	8. Thomas	8. Matthew
9. James/Alph	9. James/Alph	9. James/Alph	9. James/Alph
10. Thadeus	10. Thaddeus	10. Simon/Zealot	10. Simon/Zealot
11. Simon/Zealot	11. Simon/Zealot	11. Judas/son of James	11. Judas/son of James — Thaddeus
12. Judas Iscariot	12. Judas Isc.	12. Judas Iscar.	12.

Note: Thaddeus also went by the name Judas, son of James.

Who is always listed first? Peter

Who is listed last in Matthew's, Mark's, and Luke's lists, and what is said about him? Judas Iscariot

Who is missing from the list in Acts? Judas Iscariot

In all four passages, the groups of four remain the same, and the groups are always given in the same order. Although the order in which the disciples are named changes slightly within some of the groups of four, the placements within the first and last groups give us clues about the disciple who received the most honor and the one who was least on the list.

145

The biblical authors couldn't resist listing Judas last every time. In the lists from three of the Gospels, they give away the end of the story by telling us from the very moment the disciples are chosen that Judas will betray Jesus. Acts doesn't name him at all since his story had already come to an end.

The first group of disciples is the list of the four who were closest to Jesus—two sets of brothers who were the first disciples Jesus called. And always at the top of that list, always named first in the first group, is Simon Peter. His position at the top of the list marks him as the leader and spokesperson of the disciples. The rough, impetuous fisherman is an unlikely but clear selection to lead the disciples and the future church.

Simon leads the group in many of the Gospel stories. Sometimes his leadership is intentional, planned, and strategic. Sometimes it seems almost accidental—an inadvertent byproduct of his reckless, impulsive nature. Sometimes the other disciples seem to hang back, letting Simon stick his neck out and take the risks they don't want to take.

Although his risky behavior sometimes gets him in trouble, there are times when he lands on the right answer, almost by accident. Never was that more true than on the day that Jesus changed Simon's name. Jesus was giving His disciples a pop quiz. He first asked them: "Who do others say that I am?" It was easy to tell Jesus what they had overheard from the crowds of people around them.

Once they had passed the easy portion of the test, Jesus asked them: "Who do *you* say that I am?" It was one of those questions that required them to think about all they had heard and seen in their time with Jesus, to put the facts together, and then to create an answer that matched their experiences, observations, beliefs, and feelings about Jesus. They all hesitated at that point. All of them, that is, except Simon.

I doubt that Simon stopped to think about what the other disciples would think or if he had the right answer or an answer that Jesus would like. In keeping with his impulsive nature, he probably went with his gut and simply reacted.

Reread Matthew 16:16 and fill in the blanks:

Simon Peter answered, "You are the Messiah *, the* Son *of the living* God *." (NIV)*

No one had told Simon that Jesus was the Messiah (the Christ), the One that all of Israel had awaited for so long. He seemed to blurt it out in a moment of passion. And for once it was just the right thing to say.

Jesus isn't interested in what we've overheard about Him from others. He wants to know what we think and believe about Him ourselves. You can tell Jesus what your parents say about Him, what your pastors and church leaders

> Jesus isn't interested in what we've overheard about Him from others. He wants to know what we think and believe about Him ourselves.

say about Him, what you've read about Him in books or overheard about Him from friends or acquaintances, and He'll still keep asking: "But who do you say that I am?"

Imagine that Jesus is standing before you now, asking, "Who do you say that I am?" What is *your* answer? How would you express it to Him?

The messiah, the CHRIST — THE ONE SENT FOR ME FROM GOD!

Simon was transparent, honest, and personal in his response. Instead of speaking from a carefully measured academic lecture or religious sermon, he spoke from his heart. And he acknowledged that Jesus was the One he personally had been waiting for, the One who was changing His life and could change the world. Jesus rewarded Simon with a response that must have stunned the other disciples:

> *Jesus replied, "Blessed are you, Simon son of Jonah, for this was not revealed to you by man, but by my Father in heaven. And I tell you that you are Peter, and on this rock I will build my church, and the gates of Hades will not overcome it."*
>
> Matthew 16:17-18

According to Jesus, who revealed this to Simon?

Our Father in heaven

The name Simon means "He Hears and Obeys." This name had hung around his neck like an oversized sweater that never quite fit. He never really listened much. He was too busy blurting out the first thing on his mind. And obedience? That continued to be a struggle for him throughout the Gospel stories.

Based on what you read in verse 18, what did his new name, Peter, mean?

Rock

The name Peter means "Rock, Boulder." It describes a solid foundation. At first it doesn't seem any more appropriate than the name he had before. But what Jesus says next tells us something about His reasoning for choosing this impetuous follower to lead the pack.

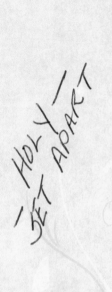

What did Jesus say He would do in verse 18?

The phrase "I will build" means that Jesus was willing to call someone who was a work in progress, someone on whom He could build a vision, a foundation for the future of His church. Jesus is claiming Simon because he was great building material, not because he was a finished product.

The reasons God is attracted to us as followers—the magnetic pull to do everything in His power to make us one of His own—has nothing to do with anything we've already built ourselves up to be. It has everything to do with His unconditional love for us just as we are.

Read Romans 5:6-8. When did God commit the ultimate act of love for us, and what does that prove?

CHRIST died for the ungodly — But GOD demonstrates His own love for us — While we are still sinners, CHRIST died for us.

The most muddled personality in Jesus' hands is worth more in the kingdom of God than the person who seems to have it all together but denies God access and authority in her or his life. Peter is living proof of that!

Aren't you glad God calls us just the way we are? If He waited for us to become perfect in order to qualify us for His band of followers, He would be waiting forever. We simply don't have the ability to make ourselves good enough for God, so God comes to us where we are. He scoops us up as if we were a rare and precious asset, while those around us shake their heads wondering what He sees in us. Amid the world's choruses of "That one will never be a saint!" God enjoys proving them wrong.

Pray About It

Jesus, we are so grateful that You aren't looking for perfection. Thank You that You love us just the way we are, and that You choose us to follow You not because of our own efforts but because of Your deep and unconditional love for us. We offer ourselves to You as raw material. Build on our flaws until they become strengths. Make us leaders so that more people can follow You and experience Your grace. Amen.

Act on It

- In the space below, make a list of the most effective leaders <u>you have</u> known. Next to their names, list the characteristics that make them great.

[handwritten: Personally]

[handwritten: In my Past: MY HUSBAND — MY BROTHER — My Grandfather — PUT THEIR LIVES ON THE LINE FOR our COUNTRY

Scott — being real + vulnerable to show us the WAY —

Jim Bell Teachers — not Preachers]

- Now write your own name. God chooses you to be His follower and a leader of others in His kingdom! Ask God what He loves and treasures about you, and list those things here.

[handwritten: — DEB — That I LOVE PEOPLE, my FAMILY — Try to FOLLOW HIM]

Day 2: Slow-Cooker Change

Read God's Word

[21] From that time on Jesus began to explain to his disciples that he must go to Jerusalem and suffer many things at the hands of the elders, the chief priests and the teachers of the law, and that he must be killed and on the third day be raised to life.

[22] Peter took him aside and began to rebuke him. "Never, Lord!" he said. "This shall never happen to you!"

[23] Jesus turned and said to Peter, "Get behind me, Satan! You are a stumbling block to me; you do not have in mind the concerns of God, but merely human concerns."

Matthew 16:21-23

Reflect and Respond

I'm a journaler. On the top shelf of my closet is a box filled with old notebooks and journals going back to the third grade. Each one contains my thoughts—from profound to childish—recording what was going on in my life in an attempt to make sense of it. Writing things down often has a way of bringing clarity to our experiences. Sometimes simply writing out our confusion or struggles can bring a solution to light that we hadn't thought of before.

Those written records of our lives and thoughts can bring a different kind of gift when we go back and read them months or years later. I love looking through some of my early notebooks from middle school and high school. They're filled with tales of the battles in teenage friendships, scribblings about boys I liked, and lists of what I was hoping to grow up to be someday. Later journals remind me of the spiritual struggles of young adulthood, working to let go of childish ways and allow God to transform me.

One thing those journals reveal is the way history repeats itself. Often I fight with the same temptations and struggles from one year to the next. In one notebook I promise God that I've learned my lesson, but when I open the next journal I find I've fallen into the same potholes again. I'd love to say that my life with God has been one of constant improvement, but my life is sometimes better described as two steps forward and one step back. The proof is there in my own handwriting.

If you could go back through journals describing your life experiences over the years, what themes would repeat themselves?

TRUSTING + BREAKING AWAY — ONLY TO COME BACK AND TRY AGAIN

Peter's story reads like a journal of life's ups and downs. If we could read the stories about him in the Gospels from *his* point of view, we would likely hear about his excitement and apprehension upon leaving his whole life behind to follow Jesus. We would learn how his world was shaken when Jesus changed his name to "Rock" and declared that he would use him as a foundation on which to build the church. But right alongside his exhilaration and accomplishment, we'd also hear of his setbacks, the way his flaws tended to rear their ugly heads again and again.

If we could read Peter's own journals through the years, we would see that some of the same struggles he had before meeting Jesus popped up again in the years that followed. Like most of us, his old life seemed to follow him like a shadow. He possessed both a desire to change and a resistance to change that makes his life resemble a spiritual yo-yo. While Peter did change and grow as he walked with Jesus, the same flaws he had as a brash fisherman when Jesus called him beside the sea were still present even after he became the leader of the disciples.

Yesterday we read about Peter's transforming, name-changing moment when he declared Jesus to be the Messiah and Jesus declared him to be the Rock on which the church would be built. But today, as we continue reading in the same chapter of Matthew, the story immediately following Peter's high point shows us one of his deepest valleys.

In your Bible, look up Matthew 16. Notice that there is only one verse separating the passage you read yesterday (Matthew 16:13-20) from today's passage (Matthew 16:21-23).

Read Matthew 16:13-20. Then read Matthew 16:21-23.

How would you describe the atmosphere of each passage? Jesus BLESSES Peter But then Peter did not want to let Jesus suffer what was to come — Get behind me Satan.

How do you think Peter felt at the end of each passage? Blessed by 6:17-19 — Saddened by 6:21-23

Peter's first outburst meant that he recognized Jesus as the Messiah when others (even those close to Jesus) had no clue. Peter's second, disruptive outburst had him standing squarely in Jesus' path, blocking the way to God's mission on earth. Although God's people had been waiting and hoping for a Messiah for thousands of years, their understanding of what the Messiah would do never included suffering or death by crucifixion, something reserved for the most scandalous criminals.

What was Jesus explaining to the disciples in Matthew 16:21? Having to go to Jerusalem and suffer many things at the hands of the elders

Why do you think Peter reacted the way he did? Surprised — Sad — Not wanting to believe it — LoVED Jesus

What did Jesus say was the source of Peter's point of view in verse 23? Get behind me Satan — You are a stumbling block — you do not have the concerns of GOD but merely man.

How does that contrast with the source of Peter's knowledge in the previous passage (v. 17)? BUILDING HIS CHURCH — Being told to GET Behind me Satan —

Read Isaiah 55:8-9. What do these verses say about the difference between the mind of God and the minds of people? HIS ways are not our ways — thoughts are Higher

"For my thoughts are not your thoughts, neither are your ways my ways," declares the LORD. "As the heavens are higher than the earth, so are my ways higher than your ways and my thoughts than your thoughts."
Isaiah 55:8-9

Understanding what Has to COME —

151

Just as quickly as Peter became the hero of the day through his understanding of Jesus' identity as Messiah, his misunderstanding of the role of Messiah instantly made him a hindrance to God's mission. In that moment the Rock that was meant to be a foundation for Jesus' message became a stumbling block. Peter learned in that moment that his words not only could make him a mouthpiece for God; they also could make him a tool of Satan, a stumbling block standing in the way of the very calling that Jesus had come to earth to fulfill.

That had to be a low blow, going from your Savior calling you Rock to referring to you as Satan. The noun and proper name Satan is actually derived from a Hebrew verb meaning "to obstruct" or "to oppose." When Peter thought he was doing Jesus a favor by telling him he would never suffer and die in such a horrible manner, he was actually obstructing Jesus' path, putting himself in the way of Jesus' ultimate purpose on earth.

And that's only the first time in Scripture that we see Peter reverting back to his old ways.

At the Last Supper, in a shocking act of servanthood, Jesus offered to wash the disciples' feet. Instead of celebrating the moment or waiting to see what Jesus might be trying to teach him, Peter recoiled and rebuked Jesus: "'No!' [he] said. 'You will never wash my feet!'" (John 13:8 CEB).

Note that when Jesus explained His purpose in washing their feet, Peter begged for Jesus to wash all of him (John 13:9). Again his impulsivity brought to light both the worst and the best in his heart.

You may have noticed that the Bible often uses Peter's old and new names interchangeably, even after Jesus elevated him to rocklike status with his name change. The truth is that sometimes Peter lived up to his new name. Other times he acted more like his pre-Jesus self. At those times Jesus called him Simon, pointing out that he was acting like his old self and not the Rock that Jesus had called him to become.

Read Mark 14:37. What was Peter doing here when Jesus called him Simon?
Sleeping

What argument did Jesus interrupt between the disciples (including Peter) at the Last Supper in Luke 22:24? What corrective instruction does Jesus give them in Luke 22:26? Not to be like benefactors — to be like youngest — as one who serves —

Immediately following the disciples' argument, how many times did Jesus call Peter the name Simon in Luke 22:31?
2 X's

Simon Peter is a hybrid of his two names, which also appears in Scripture, reminding us (and him) that transformation doesn't happen overnight—that often we are living with both our old nature and our new hope, all in one self.

When it comes to transformation in our lives, most of us would love a microwave solution, one where we could watch change unfolding quickly through a little window. Sometimes that happens. I've known people who have experienced freedom from a lifelong temptation or have been transformed in just one moment. More often though, God works with us in the slow movement of grace that takes a lifetime.

Sometimes we have the idea that a life committed to Christ will be instantly better. This leads people to the expectation that the moment their lives are in Jesus' hands, they won't struggle anymore—that their flaws will melt away and their temptations will fade. That way of thinking is similar to the idea that many people have about marriage—that saying "I do" will automatically transform the couple into new persons. We say it all the time: "You just need to find someone and settle down," as if getting married will automatically settle you down— make you more stable, more dependable, more mature. A lot of people find out the hard way that the only thing getting married makes you is married. You have to work at the growing up part together.

Likewise, the only thing giving your life to Christ makes you is a Christian. All the same temptations, all the same struggles, all the same character flaws that drove you into the arms of Christ will follow you there. The difference is that Jesus is there to help you with all of it. Jesus is the One with the power to enable each of us to live a transformed life.

Sanctification, the process of change that makes us more and more like Jesus, is more like a slow cooker than a microwave. Even as we walk with God, we sometimes will fall down again, often in the same potholes we fell into before. But there is always hope and grace and forgiveness. Thank God He has the patience and grace to work on us over the long haul, when we would have given up on ourselves long ago.

Where do you see "slow-cooker change" in your own life?
How has God helped you to change over time?

The change is there, though it may be barely perceptible at times. We'd like to see a lightning-fast transformation. But we need to remember that the process of change we are going through is as important as the end result itself.

> All the same temptations, all the same struggles, all the same character flaws that drove you into the arms of Christ will follow you there. The difference is that Jesus is there to help you with all of it.

What do the following passages say about the process of our transformation?

Romans 12:1-2 *Offer our bodies to GOD —*

2 Corinthians 3:17-18 *The LORD IS The Spirit — Freedom — We are being transformed into HIS image ever increasing glory.*

Peter's journey is characterized by ups and downs along the way. Sometimes he shows his rocklike faith by <u>walking on water to meet Jesus</u>. Sometimes he sinks like a stone. But as we follow his life, we'll find that he does change and grow and ultimately live into the name Jesus has given him.

Your journey likely has ups and downs as well. Sometimes you may look like a poster child for the changes faith can bring. Other times you may find yourself <u>sinking back into your old habits</u>. Up or down, know that <u>God is with you</u>, and that <u>His love for you does not change with the whims of your behavior</u>. He is writing a new story for your life, and that story has grace spelled out on every page.

Pray About It

Lord, help us to be as patient with ourselves as You are with us. As we walk this path with You, remind us that we are being transformed into Your likeness with ever-increasing glory. Show us the points of glory, the places where we have grown and changed, and help us long to be more like You every day. Amen.

Amen!

> [God] is writing a new story for your life, and that story has grace spelled out on every page.

Act on It

- Graph your journey with God in the space below, indicating the high points, the low points, and the times in between. Write or illustrate what was going on at these times in your life. Is your graph one of steadily climbing spiritual growth, or does it look more like a roller coaster with ups and downs? Reflect on the role that setbacks have played in your journey.

Totally a Rollercoaster

Day 3: Disappointing God

Read God's Word

[31] "Simon, Simon, Satan has asked to sift you as wheat. [32] But I have prayed for you, Simon, that your faith may not fail. And when you have turned back, strengthen your brothers."

[33] But he replied, "Lord, I am ready to go with you to prison and to death."

[34] Jesus answered, "I tell you, Peter, before the rooster crows today, you will deny three times that you know me."

Luke 22:31-34

[54] Then seizing him, they led him away and took him into the house of the high priest. Peter followed at a distance. [55] But when they had kindled a fire in the middle of the courtyard and had sat down together, Peter sat down with them. [56] A servant girl saw him seated there in the firelight. She looked closely at him and said, "This man was with him."

[57] But he denied it. "Woman, I don't know him," he said.

[58] A little later someone else saw him and said, "You also are one of them."

"Man, I am not!" Peter replied.

155

⁵⁹ *About an hour later another asserted, "Certainly this fellow was with him, for he is a Galilean."*

⁶⁰ *Peter replied, "Man, I don't know what you're talking about!" Just as he was speaking, the rooster crowed.* ⁶¹ *The Lord turned and looked straight at Peter. Then Peter remembered the word the Lord had spoken to him: "Before the rooster crows today, you will disown me three times."* ⁶² *And he went outside and wept bitterly.*

Luke 22:54-62

Reflect and Respond

A while back I had an encounter with a friend that left me feeling hurt and betrayed. For several years we had enjoyed a close friendship that was a fun mix of personal and professional. We could easily shift back and forth from working together on a large project to laughing over lunch to spending time with each other's families. Then one day my friend came in, red in the face, upset about some differences we had. He let me know that our friendship was over. The professional relationship would still be there, he said, but he was "backing off" from any contact we had beyond that. I was stunned, apologized for my part of the rift, and tried to offer a way to rebuild our friendship. His cold response let me know that wasn't an option. I was hurt—and deeply disappointed.

I hate it when people I rely on disappoint me: when a friend promises to help me with something and then blows it off; when a babysitter backs out at the last minute; when someone's attitude or reaction is far beneath what I had come to expect from him or her. Even worse than being disappointed is the feeling of disappointing someone else: when I realize an e-mail has gone unanswered or a call has gone unreturned for so long that someone assumes I just don't care; when I forget someone's special day because my life is running so fast I lose track of anyone else's concerns but my own. I hate letting people down. And I really hate the feeling of being disappointed in myself. In a perfect world there would be no disappointment.

There would also be no mosquitoes. No taxes. No rush-hour traffic. In a perfect world there would be no fights to get teenagers to do their homework, since there definitely would be no homework! In a perfect world our bodies wouldn't fall apart as we get older. We wouldn't have to say goodbye to the ones we love. Our hearts wouldn't sting from the disappointment of broken relationships. But we don't live in a perfect world, do we?

We could, you know, if it weren't for those infamous ancestors of ours: Adam and Eve. They had the perfect world, Eden, and they traded it all away for a snack that they believed would benefit them. (And it wasn't even chocolate!)

They handed over the keys to Eden because of a piece of fruit.

Genesis describes Eden as a place of wholeness, where relationships between people were without flaw. Adam and Eve are described as "naked and unashamed," which among other things means that they had nothing to hide from one another or from God. Before they messed up, they never hurt or disappointed each other. They never experienced shame or guilt.

The moments when I long for Eden the most are the ones when brokenness is the most obvious—when sickness, pain, death, divorce, destruction, war, and even disappointment mar the landscape of this once perfect world. Sometimes I think about all that we're missing out on because Adam and Eve felt the need to have a little bite. But I also wonder if there's anything we *do* have in this post-Eden world that we never would have known had the human race always existed inside the garden of perfection. Is there any benefit of living in this imperfect world?

I think it's this: we get to see how God deals with disappointment. If Adam and Eve had never touched that forbidden fruit (and, let's face it, if they hadn't, someone to come in their family line would have), then we never would have seen how God handles less than perfect lives, messy relationships, and disobedient children.

When God discovered that His children had done exactly what He told them not to do, I'm sure He experienced an immediate sinking feeling of disappointment. I mean, there were a million good choices available, but they picked the one thing that would hurt the Father who had given them everything. God's disappointment is not like our own. Our disappointment is usually self-centered, focused on our unrealized expectations. God's disappointment is always selfless, focused on the damage we cause to our own lives and to our relationship with Him. When God is disappointed with our actions, it is because He wants the absolute best for us. God loves us too much to let anything stand in the way of the wonderful future He envisions for us, even if that thing is something of our own choosing. God's disappointment in Eden was with a choice that would now shift the entire future of humanity.

But I wonder if, alongside that feeling of disappointment, there was a little bit of excitement in God's heart—a feeling of joy that He would get to show us a part of Himself we never would have known had we stuck to the straight and narrow. I wonder if God rolled up His sleeves and thought: "All right. Now I get to show them what I'm really made of." And this is what God is made of: grace.

When Adam and Eve rocked our world by defying God, when they tried to dethrone God and put themselves in His place as the One whose plans are best for the universe, God was deeply disappointed. And yet God responded with grace.

We call that first story of sin "the Fall" of humanity, but every generation since has fallen again on its own. If we're honest, we must admit that we don't usually

God loves us too much to let anything stand in the way of the wonderful future He envisions for us.

fall into sin; we willfully throw ourselves headlong into it. Each generation has its own experience of disappointing God. And in each generation God responds with grace. He reaches out, offering Himself again and again. Even when He knows we will grieve His heart again, God still shows up full of grace.

What do these verses teach us about God's grace?

Ephesians 2:8-9 *We are saved by GRACE through FAITH —*

Hebrews 4:16 *Finding grace in our time of need.*

Romans 5:1-2 *Death through Adam — LIFE THROUGH CHRIST*

No one needed God's grace more than Peter. We've already seen Peter's pattern of ups and downs throughout his walk with Jesus. Now let's look at how Jesus responded—how He handled disappointment.

The order that events are shared in a specific Gospel often has meaning. We've seen how quickly Peter's high point in Matthew 16:17-18 was followed by his low point in Matthew 16:23. What would we expect to happen next? For Peter to be kicked out of the group? Demoted from the position of leader?

What happened next according to Matthew 17:1-3?
— The transfiguration —

Who was present? *Peter, James, John (Brother of James) MOSES + ELIJAH —*

It's clear that Jesus didn't give up on Peter; instead, He continued to invite him into His inner circle, even bringing Peter with Him in the select group of disciples who had the amazing privilege of witnessing what we have come to call the Transfiguration, a moment of Jesus' heavenly glory on earth.

Now let's look more closely at Peter's "double Simon" moment, when Jesus admonished him by using his old name not once, but twice.
— SIMON —

Read Luke 22:31-34. What did Jesus tell Peter that Satan had asked to do (v. 31)?
SIFT ALL AS ~~SIFT~~ wheat

> *Let us then approach God's throne of grace with confidence, so that we may receive mercy and find grace to help us in our time of need.*
> Hebrews 4:16

What did Jesus tell Peter that He had done (v. 32)? *Jesus Prayed for Simon that his faith may not fail —*

Sifting wheat is an act of separating the useful part (kernel) from the junk (chaff). The whole of the wheat is shaken in a sieve. The good kernels stay firmly in the mesh while the chaff either falls through the cracks or flies up and floats away, too light to stay firmly planted with the pieces of substance. Sifting implies separating the good from the bad, the substance from the rubbish.

The interesting thing here is that the "you" in both of these sentences is plural. Where I'm from, we would translate it "y'all." Jesus was talking about all of the disciples in these two sentences, not just Peter. Here's the Texas translation: "Satan has asked to sift y'all like wheat. But I have prayed for y'all, Simon, that your faith may not fail."

Peter puffed himself up with characteristic bravado and declared that he was ready to face prison or even death for Jesus' sake. He was asserting that he would never be the one to betray Jesus, to turn away from his loyalty, to disappoint the Savior he loved. Jesus knew better.

What did Jesus predict Peter would do in Luke 22:34? *deny 3 X's before the Rooster crowed!*

Now read Luke 22:54-62. How accurate was Jesus' prediction? *— Total*

According to Luke 22:32, what did Jesus predict Peter would do when all was said and done? *Faith not fail — Turn back + Strengthen your brothers*

Peter's disappointing behavior was not a surprise to Jesus. It didn't catch Him off guard. It didn't make Him love Peter any less. Jesus actually reached out in grace before Peter ever sinned, praying for Peter and the other disciples because He knew the toughest test of their faith—the crucifixion and death of the Savior they followed—lay only hours ahead of them.

Jesus knew that Peter would disappoint Him by denying Him. But He also knew that Peter wouldn't stay down long. He prayed that this moment of struggle would be one that would strengthen Peter, and that when He bounced back He would strengthen His brothers as well.

When we act in disappointing ways, God is not surprised. He knows us better than we know ourselves, and He is ready to respond with grace. He also knows

> When we act in disappointing ways, God is not surprised. He knows us better than we know ourselves, and He is ready to respond with grace.

159

that failure is like a sieve that can strengthen us—and that those who bounce back are substance, not chaff. Jesus has ordered the world so that the strengthened become the strengtheners—so that we not only learn from our moments of disappointing God but also enable others to learn from them as well.

Why did the gospel writers include this unfortunate story of the leader of the disciples denying his Messiah and closest friend? Because it can strengthen our faith, too. Our failures, our moments of disappointing God, aren't meant to be kept in the dark as secret moments of shame. We can bring them out in the light as testimonies for others to see God's gracious and forgiving nature in the face of disappointment.

Read 1 John 2:12. Why have we been forgiven?

Reasons for writing

Some translations say that we have been forgiven "for His name's sake." Others say we have been forgiven "on account of his name"—in other words, to make a name for God, to advertise that God is gracious and merciful, even when our actions are crushing. Eden may have been a perfect world, but the one thing it didn't have was forgiveness—the ability to meet disappointment not by recoiling or lashing out but by offering grace.

I long for that perfect world sometimes. But if humanity had stayed there, we never would have known how God deals with disappointment. Just as we have a choice, God has a choice. He could choose to reject us or to offer us a cold shoulder. Instead, I believe God rolls up His sleeves with a sense of excitement: "Now I get to show them what I'm really made of." We'll find out in tomorrow's reading just how God chose to pour out grace to Peter.

When my friend hurt me, I had a choice. I have to admit that it was tempting to withdraw, to lick my wounds, to pretend that our friendship never mattered to me in the first place. Instead, I am choosing daily to respond to disappointment with the same enthusiasm as Jesus. If my friend had never hurt me, I never would have had a chance to show what I'm truly made of as a child of God: grace.

When others disappoint you, you have a chance to respond by showing the nature of God in a completely new way. In a perfect world, that part of God's nature in you would remain hidden. Instead, let grace give you away.

I am writing to you, dear children, because your sins have been forgiven on account of his name.
1 John 2:12

Pray About It

God, we're disappointed in the way others have hurt us and those we love. Some of those disappointments are small and insignificant. Others are so big they feel like a heavy weight on our shoulders. Help us to be thankful for this chance to show what we're made of. Teach us to respond as You do, with grace and mercy. And when we are the ones doing the disappointing, help us to be quick to ask for forgiveness and quick to forgive ourselves. Amen.

Act on It

- **List below the names of some people who have disappointed or hurt you in the past. Start with personal relationships, but expand to companies, institutions, people groups, or organizations that have disappointed you in some way. Circle one or two that you'd like to work on forgiving. Brainstorm ways you can respond to each of these with joy, showing what you're made of by displaying the nature of Christ.**

Day 4: God's Arithmetic

Read God's Word

¹ Afterward Jesus appeared again to his disciples, by the Sea of Tiberias. It happened this way: ² Simon Peter, Thomas (called Didymus), Nathanael from Cana in Galilee, the sons of Zebedee, and two other disciples were together. ³ "I'm going out to fish," Simon Peter told them, and they said, "We'll go with you." So they went out and got into the boat, but that night they caught nothing.

⁴ Early in the morning, Jesus stood on the shore, but the disciples did not realize that it was Jesus.

⁵ He called out to them, "Friends, haven't you any fish?"

"No," they answered.

⁶ He said, "Throw your net on the right side of the boat and you will find some." When they did, they were unable to haul the net in because of the large number of fish.

⁷ Then the disciple whom Jesus loved said to Peter, "It is the Lord!" As soon as Simon Peter heard him say, "It is the Lord," he wrapped his outer garment around him (for he had taken it off) and jumped into the water. ⁸ The other disciples followed in the boat, towing the net full of fish, for they were not far from shore, about a hundred yards. ⁹ When they landed, they saw a fire of burning coals there with fish on it, and some bread.

¹⁰ Jesus said to them, "Bring some of the fish you have just caught."

¹¹ Simon Peter climbed aboard and dragged the net ashore. It was full of large fish, 153, but even with so many the net was not torn. ¹² Jesus said to them, "Come and have breakfast." None of the disciples dared ask him, "Who are you?" They knew it was the Lord. ¹³ Jesus came, took the bread and gave it to them, and did the same with the fish. ¹⁴ This was now the third time Jesus appeared to his disciples after he was raised from the dead.

¹⁵ When they had finished eating, Jesus said to Simon Peter, "Simon son of John, do you truly love me more than these?"

"Yes, Lord," he said, "you know that I love you."

Jesus said, "Feed my lambs."

¹⁶ Again Jesus said, "Simon son of John, do you truly love me?"

He answered, "Yes, Lord, you know that I love you."

Jesus said, "Take care of my sheep."

¹⁷ The third time he said to him, "Simon son of John, do you love me?"

Peter was hurt because Jesus asked him the third time, "Do you love me?" He said, "Lord, you know all things; you know that I love you."

Jesus said, "Feed my sheep. ¹⁸ I tell you the truth, when you were younger you dressed

yourself and went where you wanted; but when you are old you will stretch out your hands, and someone else will dress you and lead you where you do not want to go." ¹⁹*Jesus said this to indicate the kind of death by which Peter would glorify God. Then he said to him, "Follow me!"*

John 21:1-19

Reflect and Respond

I hesitate to tell strangers what I do for a living. People traditionally clam up when I tell them I'm a pastor. Something about standing next to a representative of God makes them think of all the things they've done wrong or all the Sundays they've slept in instead of going to church.

I thought I was the only one who was hesitant to tell people what I did for a living. Then I met my husband, Jim. When we first started dating, he had been a math professor for several years. When Jim would tell people that he taught math, their response was almost inevitably negative: "I hated math in school!" It wasn't exactly a great conversation starter. We were quite the life of the party—the preacher and the math professor!

The mere mention of Jim's profession caused most people to reflect on how inadequate they felt the last time they sat in math class struggling over an algebra problem or stood at the chalkboard fearing the ridicule of their classmates as they tried to solve a differential equation. Math brought back bad memories for people.

Honestly, we both learned not to take it personally when people scowled within minutes of meeting us. In a way, the reasons behind the reactions people had to our professions weren't that different. The negative experiences of the past still left a bad impression in their minds that caused a shudder at just the mention of God or church or arithmetic.

You know, God and arithmetic actually can be a winning combination, because God's arithmetic is a freeing thing.

When Jesus took away Simon's old name and gave him a new one, it wasn't so much an act of subtraction. Jesus' renaming of Simon was more an exercise in addition. While some other individuals whose names changed lost their old names for good (Abraham, for example, was never called Abram again once God gave him a new name), you may have noticed that Simon Peter kept his old name throughout much of his story.

We've already noticed that, though he is referred to as Peter often in Scripture, there were times Jesus called him out on his pre-conversion behavior by calling him by his old name. There were even more times, though, when he was referred to as Simon Peter, a nod to his old and new nature mixed together in one. Becoming Peter didn't mean that Simon was lost.

If we're honest, most of us are also a mix of the old and the new, a work in progress with Jesus gradually helping us subtract the negative and add the positive. If we learn anything from Peter, it's that it certainly takes some time to work out our spiritual kinks.

If the disciples had been students of Jesus, learning from Him for three years, the last few days they spent with Him were definitely an accelerated course. The day before the crucifixion was like a final exam for all the disciples, but especially for Peter. He crammed more learning and life change into his last few days with Jesus than many of us can imagine absorbing in a lifetime! The story of this day is told in several of the Gospel accounts. The following Scriptures piece together some of the events.

Read each Scripture. Then put a plus or minus in the blank beside it to indicate whether you think it was a positive or negative moment for Peter.

Luke 22:14-20 _____ *The Last Supper*

Luke 22:24 _*Who is the greatest*_

Luke 22:33 _*Ready to go to prison + death*_

Luke 22:34 _*deny 3 x's*_

John 13:8 _*Peter said Jesus should never wash his feet — unless I wash you — you have no part of me*_

John 13:9 _*wash all of me not just my feet, hands + head as well*_

Mark 14:32-41 _*Gethsemane — Jesus Take this cup — disciples sleeping — The hour has come*_

John 18:10 _*Jesus arrested — Peter cut off the high priests ear. Malchus*_

Matthew 26:69-75 _*Peter disowns Jesus*_

Talk about a rough night! You can see why Peter's learning curve was so steep here at the end of his time with Jesus. And you can see God's love for numbers begin to unfold. *Falling asleep —*

What number appears again and again in Peter's story? *3*

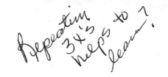
Repeating 3×'s helps to 7.

It's no accident that the number three appears over and over again in Peter's story, helping to tie the pieces together. Even though his story is recorded in fragments by the authors of all four Gospels, each of them remembered to mention the number that became very significant in Peter's story.

After Jesus asked the *three* leading disciples to stay awake and pray with Him, He returned *three* times to find them sleeping. When Jesus was arrested and dragged away to be beaten and put on trial, Peter followed at a distance. Those events must have seemed so unbelievable, so horrible. In the middle of it all, *three* different people recognized Peter as a follower of Jesus. At the very moment Jesus needed Peter's support the most, strong Peter melted into the old Simon and denied that he even knew Jesus—not once, not twice, but *three* times. His mind must have flashed back to the conversation when Jesus predicted that betrayal. The feelings of failure and shame must have been overwhelming to Peter. Not only had he let down his Savior: he had done it even after Jesus had predicted and warned him about it!

Here is where Peter needed forgiveness the most. This was his moment of greatest need, and this is where Jesus really triumphed. It's at our times of greatest need that Jesus can show us the greatest forgiveness, and forgiveness was what those few days were all about. Within hours of Peter's denial, Jesus was hanging on a cross, taking on the sins of the world. Even more important to Peter must have been the realization that Jesus was taking on *his* sins as well.

Here is where the arithmetic of God just doesn't add up to the rest of the world.

Somehow, when God is balancing the equation of grace, one innocent figure on a cross can equal forgiveness for all of humanity.

One of the ironies of God's arithmetic on the cross is that Peter already had had one math lesson in forgiveness. He was the one who sometime before had asked Jesus to set limits on forgiveness.

Read Matthew 18:21-22. What number did Peter propose for the limit of how many times he should be required to forgive?

Parable of unmerciful servant
Not 7 but 70×7

What number did Jesus give him instead?

In some translations Jesus' number is given as "seventy seven times." In others it's translated "seventy times seven." Think about it. To keep count of someone's sins against you all the way up to 490 would require some serious, grudge-bearing sin accounting! Jesus is expressing that the number of times we forgive should be more than we can even keep count of.

> When God is balancing the equation of grace, one innocent figure on a cross can equal forgiveness for all of humanity.

What does 1 Corinthians 13:5 say about keeping count of the times someone has wronged us? Love does not dishonor others, not self seeking - not easily angered - Keeps no record of wrongs

Of all the times Simon Peter should have been grateful for a math lesson, it was that one, because it turned out he was going to need it. "How many times should we forgive someone, Lord? Five, six, seven? Should I keep count on my fingers?" After denying Jesus, Peter was definitely in need of a seventy-times-seven kind of forgiveness. And the days surrounding Jesus' crucifixion and resurrection were a perfect time to see Jesus put that promise into action.

When Jesus and Peter finally met up again, things were different. Jesus, for one, had paid the price for the sins of all of humanity, risen from the dead, and conquered the grave. He had been a little busy. Peter, on the other hand, had decided to go fishing.

It's a beautiful thing, the symmetry of this story in Acts: the way that Jesus met Peter in the exact place where they had begun; the way that He gave a fishing lesson to the most seasoned fishermen and the nets were so full they almost broke. Speaking of math—this storyteller cares so much about detail that he even lets us know exactly how many fish were caught that day (John 21:11).

Reread John 21:15-17. What question did Jesus ask Peter three times in these verses? Do you LOVE me?!

Jesus reinstates Peter

What did Jesus say to Peter in verse 19?
Follow me

When Jesus called out to Peter, "Follow me," it must have felt like déjà vu. Those were the words of his original calling. Now they were the words that called him back, letting him know that Jesus wanted him to follow in the same way as he did that first day, just as much now that Jesus had seen him at his worst as in the very beginning.

"Simon, do you love me?" Jesus asked. After giving three knife-in-the-heart denials the night before Jesus died, Peter received three chances to answer this all-important question. With each question, Jesus used his old name, his original name, Simon. Using this name said: "I know who you are, and I love you anyway. I know your struggle and pain, and I know that you are your own worst enemy; and I'm still here to offer you help."

Three times he fell asleep in the garden. "Simon . . . couldn't you stay awake?" (Mark 14:37 NCV).

Three times he denied Jesus as predicted. "Simon, Satan has asked to sift . . . you like wheat" (Luke 22:31 NLT).

Three times Jesus gave him a chance to reform, repent, and answer the most personal question possible, each time using the most personal, first-name address (John 21:15-17):

"Simon son of John, do you truly love me more than these?"
"Simon son of John, do you truly love me?"
"Simon son of John, do you love me?"

Suddenly it all added up. It didn't matter to Jesus who the world said that He was; He had wanted to know, "Who do you say that I am?" It didn't matter to Him what Simon had done. He wanted to know, "Do you love me?" And three times Simon jumped at the chance to answer "Yes!"

Jesus' questions are personal. He wants our answers to be equally personal. It doesn't mater to Him what we have done. It matters to Him what we believe about Him and how we answer the question "Do you love me?"

I often stumble, showing my old colors beneath all the work Jesus has done in me. I tell Jesus "Never!" when I should say, "Anything you ask, Lord." I fall asleep when I should be standing by Him. I betray and deny Him not once but over and over. And yet He still finds the sum of my behavior to be nothing compared to His great love and sacrifice for me.

For every mistake you make, Jesus adds one more chance. He doesn't subtract His grace or mercy. He doesn't take away the chance of a fresh start. He continually goes before you and asks you to follow Him. If you betray Him seven times, He gives you eight chances to redeem yourself. If you mess up seventy-times-seven times, God's arithmetic responds with seventy-times-seven-plus-one offers of forgiveness, followed by an invitation just like the first: "Follow me."

Jesus always offers us another chance to answer that singularly most important question: "Do you love me?"

Yes, Lord. A thousand times, yes!

Pray About It

Dear Jesus, we are so grateful for the way you handle the ups and downs of our lives. While we are all over the map with our thoughts, actions, and responses, You are the same yesterday, today, and forever. Thank You for Your patience when I need to be forgiven again and again. Help me to have the same patience, the same grace, when dealing with other people in my life. And, Lord, in response to Your question "Do you love me?" we answer "Yes, yes, yes!" Amen.

> Jesus always offers us another chance to answer that singularly most important question: "Do you love me?"

Act on It

- Is there someone in your community who is branded by an act he or she participated in that hurt one person or a group of people? Maybe it's someone you know personally who is still struggling to forgive himself or herself, or someone you've only read about or heard about that has caused pain to others. Commit to pray for the person this week. If it seems appropriate, find a way to reach out and extend grace, even if it's just a quick "hello."

Day 5: Revelation—Pray in My Name

Read God's Word

⁵ Thomas said to him, "Lord, we don't know where you are going, so how can we know the way?"

⁶ Jesus answered, "I am the way and the truth and the life. No one comes to the Father except through me. ⁷ If you really knew me, you would know my Father as well. From now on, you do know him and have seen him."

⁸ Philip said, "Lord, show us the Father and that will be enough for us."

⁹ Jesus answered: "Don't you know me, Philip, even after I have been among you such a long time? Anyone who has seen me has seen the Father. How can you say, 'Show us the Father'? ¹⁰ Don't you believe that I am in the Father, and that the Father is in me? The words I say to you are not just my own. Rather, it is the Father, living in me, who is doing his work. ¹¹ Believe me when I say that I am in the Father and the Father is in me; or at least believe on the evidence of the miracles themselves. ¹² I tell you the truth, anyone who has faith in me will do what I have been doing. He will do even greater things than these, because I am going to the Father. ¹³ And I will do whatever you ask in my name, so that the Son may bring glory to the Father. ¹⁴ You may ask me for anything in my name, and I will do it."

John 14:5-14

Reflect and Respond

When I was growing up, I had a picture of Jesus in my head when I prayed. He looked a lot like the pictures in the children's Bible that was always in the waiting room at my dentist's office. He was kind and loving, with soft brown hair and big eyes, and he listened intently when I talked. When I had tough moments, I imagined him physically walking beside me and holding my hand as I encountered things that made me worried or scared. Holding onto that image in prayer helped me through a lot of difficult experiences. But sometimes this passive, listening Jesus was easy to ignore when I wanted to do things my own way. I forgot at times that the kindness of God is also wrapped in holiness, and that God has expectations for me and desires for my life to change.

My mom tells me that while she was growing up, her picture of God was anything but kind and loving. She pictured an old man with a harsh expression, constantly looking over her shoulder, waiting for her to mess up. When she did, He was the last person she would want to go to for help. She was afraid He would judge or punish her. It wasn't until her adult years that she learned the unapproachable God she had imagined in childhood had come to earth as a very approachable person in the flesh. The Jesus she experienced as her faith matured offered her compassion and understanding, especially since He experienced all the same trials and temptations that we do during His ministry on earth.

How would you describe the image of God that you had as a child?

Even the disciples had a hard time getting their picture of God in focus. They walked with Jesus day after day, and yet they couldn't quite comprehend who He really was or what He was trying to show them. Can we blame them? Understanding God is arguably the biggest concept a human mind can ever hope to grasp.

Philip is a perfect example. When Jesus declared that the disciples knew the Father and had seen the Father, Philip still persisted in asking: "Lord, show us the Father and that will be enough for us" (John 14:8). Jesus responded: "Don't you know me, Philip, even after I have been among you such a long time?" (John 14:9).

I often imagine Jesus asking me the same question: "Don't you know me, Jessica, even after I've been with you for so long?" After all these years of calling myself a Christian, reading the Bible, and talking with God in prayer, I still feel a little in the dark sometimes about who God is and what He wants from me.

Learning who God is takes more than reading a book or two or attending a seminar. It takes a lifetime of walking with Him and searching to know Him, and even then we will only fully know God when we stand face to face with Him. The effort to understand the character of Jesus in this lifetime was about to get even more important for the disciples, because Jesus truly upped the stakes with what He offered them next.

Reread John 14:13-14. What promise did Jesus make?

That's quite an offer! Just ask me for anything in my name and I will do it. This is the verse that has encouraged Christians through the ages to add "in Jesus' name" at the end of our prayers just before the "Amen." Some have wondered if this offer is something like a spiritual blank check—as if whatever we ask, if capped off with Jesus' name at the end, will come true.

Have you ever wished for just the right words that would guarantee a certain prayer would be answered? What was that prayer?

Remember, though, that in the Bible a name is the embodiment of someone's character. It tells the story of who the person is—his or her nature or inner compass. When Jesus invites us to pray in His name, He wants our prayers to be shaped by His character, His desires, His essence. This means that we have to be even more self-aware, asking ourselves the motivation behind our prayers. Are we praying to get what we want, or are we praying that the world will become what God wants? When we pray, do we pray to change God or that God will change us?

What makes the offer of prayer in His own name so remarkable is the history of how God's people have viewed God's name. Our study of God's self-revelation began with the people of God understanding God to be so holy, so different from them, that He was unapproachable, unnamable. They were careful not to speak His name aloud or even write it for fear that someone might accidentally pronounce it and possibly be struck dead, because God's holiness was too much for a flawed human being to even name.

When Jesus showed up, the disciples' experience of Him was so different than anyone had ever imagined God to be that they weren't sure what was going on. "Show us the Father!" Philip begged, unaware that that was exactly what Jesus had been doing all along. After all the mystery surrounding the name of God, Peter and the disciples encountered God face-to-face, embodied in human flesh in a way they could understand. Only they didn't.

Who could comprehend being on a first-name basis with God when for so many centuries naming God wasn't even an option? Knowing God's name was

"And I will do whatever you ask in my name, so that the Father may be glorified in the Son."
John 14:13

170

an amazing thing. Being asked to use it in conversation with Him as a way of having your prayers answered was unbelievable. And so many of us don't—believe it, that is.

We know better than to believe that tacking the phrase "in Jesus' name" on the end of our wish lists will make them come true. You can't wish for a new car, revenge on your enemies, world peace, or whatever and think that adding Jesus' name at the end will clinch the deal.

Praying in Jesus' name is not a formula that guarantees us the answer we want. It's a sign of intimacy, assuming that we know Him well enough to know what kind of prayer would honor His name. It's another way of saying "Thy will be done on earth as it is in heaven," since we're asking for God's will—the things that honor His name—to become visibly manifest in our world. It means that praying God's name comes with the responsibility of learning enough about who God is that we can say those words at the end of a prayer with the confidence that we know what God wants. And our understanding of God's ultimate will, His ultimate triumph over the powers of darkness, means that if we want what God wants, we will ultimately get what we want.

Read 1 John 5:13-15. How do these verses echo John 14:13-14?

What new information do we gain from the 1 John passage?

Praying in Jesus' name is as much a message to us as it is to God—a message of what prayer is really about. We don't pray to point God to our desires; we pray so that God will point us in the direction of His character, shaping us and our hearts even as we ask Him into the deepest places in our hearts.

When we pray in Jesus' name, we should ask ourselves if the prayer reflects our sincere desire to have those things that reflect Jesus' lordship, character, and love done on earth as in heaven. This is a good litmus test for our prayers. Let's walk through it together.

Write a prayer below about your current situation, needs, and concerns. Close it with the words "in Jesus' name."

Father please guide me to the right doctors and lead their hands. Continue to bring me peace during all of the procedures and please lead them to find the causes of stomach issues—not only the cancer but all of it. In Jesus Name Amen!

> Praying in Jesus' name is not a formula that guarantees us the answer we want. It's a sign of intimacy, assuming that we know Him well enough to know what kind of prayer would honor His name.

Now move through the following steps.

1. <u>Lordship</u>: **Are you asking God to be in charge of the situation? Or are you taking charge, assuming you know what's best?**

Read Luke 6:46. **What do you learn about Lordship from this verse?**

If we want to know who God is, we need to look at the life and character of Jesus. He is the ultimate self-revelation of God.

2. <u>Character</u>: **When you pray this prayer, is Jesus' character reflected in you? Is this a prayer that Jesus would pray?**

Read Matthew 20:28 and John 15:13. **What do you learn about the character of Jesus from these verses?**

3. <u>Love</u>: **Are you praying this prayer out of love for all involved? Will the fulfillment of this prayer mean that God's love is spread?**

Read John 15:9-12. **What do you learn about love from these verses?**

To go from a God whose name we're not even allowed to speak to this God who invites us to use His name every time we pray is a dramatic shift. Yet Jesus reminds us that He is a God not only to be worshipped and revered but also to be approached with our smallest needs as well as our deepest desires.

If we want to know who God is, we need to look at the life and character of Jesus. He is the ultimate self-revelation of God. When Jesus showed up on earth, it was an invitation for us to know God intimately in a way that no one had ever known Him before.

You are so precious to Him, so important, that He invites you to know Him on a first-name basis. He wants you to talk to Him about all of your burdens and joys, your hopes and dreams. And He wants you to use His name to call on the strength, power, and character of the One who overcame death when you are looking to overcome things in your own life. Thank God that He offered us His Son—and His name!

Pray About It

Jesus, thank You for offering us Your name, for wanting us to know You so well that we're on a first-name basis with You in prayer. Help us to feel so comfortable with You that we share our deepest desires, needs, hurts, and joys. We're grateful that You didn't ask us to say some ritualistic formula in prayer; You ask so much more. You ask for all of us, surrendered to You. We pray that everything we put before You would reflect Your Lordship, Your character, and Your love. In Jesus' name we pray. Amen.

Act on It

- Continue using the litmus test of lordship, character, and love with your prayers this week. If something does not pass the test, ask the Holy Spirit how to pray about this concern in light of God's character and will.

Week 5
VIDEO VIEWER GUIDE

Simon Peter answered, "You are the Christ, the Son of the living God." Jesus replied, "Blessed are you, Simon son of Jonah, for this was not revealed to you by man, but by my Father in heaven. And I tell you that you are __Peter__ *, and on this* __Rock__ *I will build my church, and the gates of Hades will not overcome it.*

Matthew 16:16-18 NIV

All the same __Temptations__, __struggles__, character flaws that drove you into the arms of Christ are going to follow you there. The difference is now you have a __SAVIOR__ to help you deal with those things.

What Scripture says about you:

You are a __child__ of God.

You are __treasure__.

You were __loved__ before you were born.

You've been __forgiven__ and set free.

You have been given a __purpose__ that only you can fill.

God looks on you daily with __compassion__ in His heart.

You bring Him such great __joy__ just by being who you are.

God calls us to __change__, to build on a __new__ __foundation__ that He sees in us.

Week 6
Unnamed

Every Name Tells a Story: Nuffy

Linda and John wanted a full house of children to love. Their daughter, Alice, was the delight of their hearts, but they were even more thrilled when they found out she was going to become a big sister. When their second little girl was born, they decided that John would name her, and he chose the name Bryce. The two little blond-haired, blue-eyed girls grew together surrounded by love. Soon Linda discovered she was expecting again, and she began to think about names. She realized something that hadn't occurred to her before: her first two children were named with the first two letters of the alphabet. Even though they hadn't begun the trend on purpose, they decided not to break it; and when their third daughter arrived, they named her Crystyl, so that the three sisters could be A, B, and C. The big family they had hoped for was growing quickly.

Despite her love for her giggling group of little girls, Linda still dreamed of having a son. It seemed she might get her chance when she found out she was pregnant again. The big day arrived and they were blessed with a bouncing baby . . . girl. D'Andra it was. Four girls seemed quite enough, so Linda and John considered their family complete.

Thinking she was done having children, Linda settled into being the mom of four wonderful daughters—until a few years later she discovered they weren't done after all! She thought that maybe this was God's way of fulfilling her dream of a little boy. It turned out that God had a sense of humor. Their fifth daughter was on the way.

Linda and John thought long and hard about what would be an appropriate name for this fifth and final girl. What name would reflect the humor they saw in God's gift of so many girls? What name would help the youngest of five sisters not to take herself too seriously? They thought carefully of names that would capture her place as the caboose in the alphabetical family line and reflect the love and laughter she would bring, and they named her . . . Enuf—as in "Enough girls!" But her name also speaks of a family with more than enough: enough love and fun and laughter to go around. Nuffy, as they called her, grew up with a lovely smile and a mischievous personality, enjoying the love and attention of her big sisters.

When people hear her name and her story, they often respond with shock and surprise and ask if she is serious. They can't believe that parents would give their little girl the name Enuf. But Nuffy loves having a name that no one else has. When asked how she feels about her name, Nuffy says, "Because my name creates a spotlight for me, all of a sudden this five-foot-three-inch girl with a big smile is not dismissed as just another sweetheart or pushover. My name gives me a voice . . . and I'm going to make the most out this blessing. I love reaching people, brightening their days, making an impression. No one else has an opportunity to spread God's story and be remembered like I do."

The sisters say they loved growing up in a family full of girls, each with her own distinct personality and approach to life. Their alphabetical names give them a sense of the bond they share in such a unique family filled with love.

Our final week together studying God's impact on our names brings closure to our study. This week we'll discover the story of a woman who was named by her past, and whose legacy is different than that of the other individuals we've studied because it is shaped by her lack of a name. Through her, we'll find that God's grace is enough—enough to reshape our lives after a rocky start; enough to change our stories and our names forever.

Day 1: Unnamed, But Not Unknown

Read God's Word

² At dawn he appeared again in the temple courts, where all the people gathered around him, and he sat down to teach them. ³ The teachers of the law and the Pharisees brought in a woman caught in adultery. They made her stand before the group ⁴ and said to Jesus, "Teacher, this woman was caught in the act of adultery. ⁵ In the Law Moses commanded us to stone such women. Now what do you say?" ⁶ They were using this question as a trap, in order to have a basis for accusing him.

John 8:2-6

Reflect and Respond

Learning someone's name is usually the first step in getting to know that person. You probably wouldn't ask about the person's occupation or family until you at least knew his or her name. You certainly wouldn't think of asking about his or her deepest hurts, wildest dreams, or closest moment to God if you had never even been properly introduced.

Somehow the Bible didn't get the memo about the etiquette of introductions. Scripture is full of some of the most famously anonymous people that ever lived. It feels awkward sometimes to read the stories of the intimate details of people's lives and never learn their identity. We often know their heart's desire, the depth of their pain, the way that Jesus changed their destiny, and yet we can't even call them by name.

We call them things such as the blind beggar, the man lowered through the roof by his friends, the woman at the well, the rich young ruler, the woman who washed Jesus' feet, the boy with the five loaves and two fish, Potiphar's wife, Lot's wife, Noah's wife, and Job's wife. They were important enough to make it into the Bible, but somehow, no one thought to catch their names. We've assigned each one a nickname based on his or her circumstances, actions, or relationships, whether good or bad.

In the following stories, what are some of the intimate details we know about the unnamed individuals? What names would you give them based on their circumstances?

2 Kings 4:1-7

Matthew 9:20-22

Mark 9:17-24

The story we'll be studying together this week is one of those anonymous stories in Scripture where we become close to a person without ever learning her name. The woman we meet in our story this week is one whose nickname—often written in Scripture in bold as a title above the first paragraph of her story—is a devastating label. Because of a mistake, a moment in her life she must not have been particularly proud of, she received a nickname that marks her in every Bible that has ever been printed. She is known only as "The Woman Caught in Adultery."

I don't know about you, but if you rewound the story of my life and picked out my worst moments, I wouldn't want to be known by them for posterity. I would hate it even more if I were to be known for the rest of history by the names that I was called or that I internally called myself during my toughest times.

This woman was dragged onstage in the opening act of her own story by a group of men who were, shall we say, a little too excited about someone else's sin. They were probably keyed up and out of breath, calling out to Jesus in animated voices: "Jesus! Here's a woman caught in the very moment of her sin! We know what the Law says should be done with a woman like this. Since you're teaching on the Law, since you think you're qualified to say what is right and wrong here, what do you say? Judge her case for us."

It's clear from the story that these men weren't interested in justice. They weren't even interested in the woman. What they are interested in is Jesus— specifically, catching Him in a trap, a theological catch-22.

If He agreed with them and with the law of Moses, saying they should stone her, He would be seizing power away from the law of Rome, and the Romans would have His head. If He said she should go free without punishment, He would be defying the law of Moses and likely would lose the respect of the crowds who had been following Him.

They had Him cornered right where they wanted Him. At the least, they could split the crowd's opinion of Him, reducing the size of His following by half. And if they were successful, they might even set in motion events that would lead not to the woman's execution, but to Jesus' own death.

If they truly had been interested in sin and law and justice, there likely would have been another person present and named in the story. Let me give you a hint. It takes two to tango! There is no being caught in the act of adultery by yourself;

so somehow in their careful plot they've caught only half of the perpetrators, letting the other go free.

Read Deuteronomy 19:15 and 17:6. What were the requirements in the law of Moses for accusing someone of breaking one of the laws or for putting someone to death?

According to Jewish law, no one could be proven guilty without the testimony of two witnesses. You couldn't just be "the woman accused of adultery" or "the woman suspected of adultery." You had to be caught in the act, and you had to be caught by two eyewitnesses. So these men must have gone to a lot of trouble to have two people catch this woman in the act while, at the same time, letting her partner slip out the back door.

The way they used her for their own agenda, shaming her in a public place (the Temple, no less) shows just how little concern they had for her as a person. It's possible that she had been treated with contempt by other men in her life, that she was all too familiar with men who used her for their own purposes without truly knowing her heart, her hurts, or even her name.

Now standing before her was one more man. Even if she didn't know much about Jesus, it was clear immediately that He was teaching in the Temple as a rabbi, a teacher of the very law that she was accused of breaking. One condemning word from Him and she'd be dragged out and stoned. A forgiving word and her life would be spared. She must have wondered what this man would do with her. Her life was in His hands.

As onlookers to her story, we have the benefit of information that our frightened, unnamed friend did not have in those anxious moments. We know the Good News that the man standing before her was different than anyone she had ever met. He wasn't only a man; He was also her Creator and her God, and He loved her more than anyone ever could.

As the old country song goes, she had been "looking for love in all the wrong places," but finally she was standing in the right place. Finally, she was standing face to face with the Source of true love. This was the one place she would find fulfillment of the deep need for love that she had sought to fill in the arms of another man who could never love her enough. And her life would never be the same.

Her story is definitely one of the most powerful anonymous stories in the Bible. She is in good company with the scores of other "players to be named later" in salvation history. The one thing they have in common is this: we don't know their names, but we know they were all changed by a powerful encounter with God.

Why incorporate their stories in the Bible? If these individuals are not "important" enough to be remembered by name, why are they even included? I believe there are some very significant reasons these stories made it into our Holy Bible, even though the names of the individuals in them did not.

1. They are included to show that every life, no matter how small, has significance to God. Jesus knew the woman in this story, and He cared about her intimately whether or not anyone else there did. That is the case with us as well.

Read Psalm 139:13-14. How long have we had worth in God's eyes?

All Scripture is God-breathed and is useful for teaching, rebuking, correcting and training in righteousness.
2 Timothy 3:16

2. They are included so that we can learn from the individuals' struggles and triumphs. This woman's very public humiliation is part of history for all to read. But so is her very public redemption and the way Jesus loved her and treated her. Our own struggles, when redeemed by Christ, can become great gifts to others who learn from them.

Read 2 Corinthians 1:3-5. According to these verses, what is one reason we go through struggles?

3. They are included to remind us that God is actually the main character in our stories, and it's His name that should be lifted up, not ours. One of the mistakes we often make is to believe that life is about us. Actually, this mistake is the root of all sin: placing ourselves at the center of the universe, where God belongs. We are all playing supporting roles in God's story. He is bigger than any of our individual stories.

Read Psalm 8:1-4. How is the main character of the universe described?

4. Maybe their names are left out so that we can put our own names "in the blank," so to speak, as we read their stories. The anonymous stories of Scripture aren't meant to be fairy tales for our entertainment; they are each meant to teach us something that we can apply to our own lives.

Read 2 Timothy 3:16. What is God's Word meant to do?

I'm so thankful that this woman's story is included in God's Word! She may have been unnamed, but she was not unknown. Jesus knew her, and He loved her. He knows and loves you, too. If you ever feel a little anonymous, unremarkable, unnoticed, know that God notices your every joy and every concern. He is specifically concerned with the specifics of your life. Before you were born, He saw you. Before anyone spoke your name, He knew you. According to Him, you are fearfully and wonderfully made.

Pray About It

God, when I start to feel unnoticed and unloved, remind me again that You care intimately about me. Let me feel Your pleasure in the little things in my everyday life. Help me to remember that You saw me before anyone else even knew of my existence, and that You have loved me from that moment. And Lord, help me to pay attention to the "anonymous" people I come across. Help me to learn their names and lift them up to You. We are grateful that we all matter to You! Amen.

Act on It

- Read Psalm 139, rephrasing some of the lines that stand out to you as if they are written about you (because they are!) by inserting your own name in place of the words *me* and *I*.

- Learn the names of the anonymous people you come across this week. Address the checker at the grocery store and the bank teller by name. If there's someone you see week after week, make sure that you learn more about this person. Find ways to help the person feel seen and known. Pray for him or her by name.

Day 2: Writing in the Sand

Read God's Word

⁶ *But Jesus bent down and started to write on the ground with his finger.* ⁷ *When they kept on questioning him, he straightened up and said to them, "If any one of you is without sin, let him be the first to throw a stone at her."* ⁸ *Again he stooped down and wrote on the ground.*

⁹ *At this, those who heard began to go away one at a time, the older ones first, until only Jesus was left, with the woman still standing there.* ¹⁰ *Jesus straightened up and asked her, "Woman, where are they? Has no one condemned you?"*

¹¹ *"No one, sir," she said.*

"Then neither do I condemn you," Jesus declared. "Go now and leave your life of sin."

John 8:6-11

³¹ *"The time is coming," declares the LORD,*
   "when I will make a new covenant
with the house of Israel
   and with the house of Judah.
³² *It will not be like the covenant*
   I made with their forefathers
when I took them by the hand
   to lead them out of Egypt,
because they broke my covenant,
   though I was a husband to them,"
   declares the LORD.
³³ *"This is the covenant I will make with the house of Israel*
   after that time," declares the LORD.
"I will put my law in their minds
   and write it on their hearts.
I will be their God,
   and they will be my people.
³⁴ *No longer will a man teach his neighbor,*
   or a man his brother, saying, 'Know the LORD,'
because they will all know me,
   from the least of them to the greatest,"
   declares the LORD.
"For I will forgive their wickedness
   and will remember their sins no more."

Jeremiah 31:31-34

183

Reflect and Respond

Tony and Karen had a storybook beginning. They met singing together in the choir at church where Tony, a baritone, kept turning around to sneak peeks at Karen in the alto section. Long talks in the church parking lot after rehearsal turned into a whirlwind courtship and engagement. The choir sang at their wedding. Everyone said they were the perfect couple. Tony was nearly twenty years her senior, but Karen felt he was the man she had been looking for all her life. They had two little boys and settled down into a life that seemed perfect to everyone on the outside looking in.

On the inside, however, things were falling apart. Tony was demanding and controlling, insisting that Karen report her whereabouts at all times and badgering her until she ended most of her friendships and activities outside the home. She felt trapped and isolated. When a man she worked with asked her one day why she looked so sad, she broke down and confided in him about her misery at home. He was warm and understanding, and she began secretly looking forward to bumping into him in the break room. When he asked if she was going to a company event out of town in a few weeks and if they could drive there together, she blushed and was flattered. A nagging thought in the back of her mind warned her to stop, but she was trying hard to ignore it.

When a couple gets married, they have to apply for a license, sign their names in agreement, and take vows—a verbal contract—before witnesses. But no one wants his or her spouse's actions in marriage to be motivated by contractual agreement. We do want our spouses to keep their marriage vows, certainly, but out of much more than obligation. We want their actions toward us to be motivated not only by duty but also by love. We want their hearts.

Even though both Tony and Karen might have been keeping the letter of the law of their marriage contract, the relationship sealed by their vows was certainly suffering. Marriage is an agreement written on more than a marriage license; it is written on the hearts of the two people who enter into it together.

If you were Karen's friend and she confided in you about what was going on in her life, what would you tell her?

As we read in Day 1, Jesus was confronted in the Temple and asked to play judge in a very sensitive case. He had been put on the spot many times in his ministry, but this one was crucial. The decision Jesus was being forced to make was, on the surface, a decision about the sentencing of a woman caught breaking her marriage covenant. Her destiny was in His hands. And as we saw yesterday, the decision He would make also would determine His own fate.

A decision to uphold the law of Moses would have half the crowd cheering and marching out into the street, filling their pockets with stones to begin an execution. But the Roman authorities, already leery of this man who could draw a crowd with His borderline revolutionary teaching, would most likely retaliate. A decision to have mercy and pardon her would have some in the crowd admiring His compassion, but the Pharisees would declare that He didn't really follow the laws of the Torah and wasn't a true man of God.

Rock. Hard place. Jesus in between.

You can bet that the crowd got quiet as they waited for Jesus' decision. The accusers who had dragged the woman before Jesus fell silent as they waited to see what He would do. One particular person listened with a special intensity, straining to hear the words that would come from this man's lips. Although a group of men had dragged her into this predicament, it was now just one man who would determine whether she lived or died. All eyes were on Jesus. But Jesus wasn't looking back at any of them. Let's pick up the story at this point.

Reread John 8:6. What was Jesus doing?

He was looking at the ground. And while they watched, "Jesus bent down and started to write on the ground with his finger" (John 8:6). This made them all even more curious. What was He writing? The text doesn't tell us.

The Greek verb used for *write* is *kategraphen*—indicating more than just doodling or drawing. It specifies that Jesus was writing words. Scholars who have studied this text have guessed, discussed, and guessed some more about what Jesus was writing on the ground.

Maybe He was writing out a list of the Ten Commandments or the sins of her accusers—so that they would recognize that none of them was above reproach. Maybe Jesus was writing out all the names of the men there who were also guilty of adultery. One particular guess I like is that Jesus might have been writing her name. He might have been humanizing this unknown woman, the one they had reduced to her sin, the one who was a pawn in their plot, the one whose life was at risk because they dragged her into the Temple to her own death-sentence trial.

If Jesus was writing her identity in the sand that day, those men accusing her would have had a hard time seeing her as an unnamed object. The One who created her and loved her was naming her before them to say, *This is not a mere creature. She is more than her sin. She is more than her mistakes. She has a name.*

185

Have you ever heard these or other explanations of what Jesus might have been writing that day—or made your own guess? What do you think He was writing?

After all of the scholarship and study and discussion of what Jesus might have written that day, all we have are just good guesses. We'll never know what He wrote.

Reread John 8:7-8. After Jesus stood up and spoke to the woman's accusers, what did He do next?

We will come back to Jesus' statement to the woman's accusers in a moment. For now, I want to draw your attention to the fact that Jesus wrote not only once but twice in this story. The second time, after Jesus diffused the conflict, He wrote while her accusers trickled away, and He stopped only after they all left.

Why all this writing in the dirt? Why does the Gospel of John even include this detail in the story if it would just leave us with more questions than answers?

It's interesting that this is the only time in the Gospels we're ever told Jesus wrote anything. We don't have a record of Him writing a book or a letter or even His name.

Outside of the Gospel stories, though, we do have images of God writing, inscribing things for us to remember through history. If we look at those other times God wrote, we might have some clues of the purpose of Jesus' writing in this story. We might be able to match the handwriting of God with the actions of Jesus in this story to find out more about what was going on.

First, there are the Ten Commandments.

Read Exodus 31:18 and fill in the blanks:

When the LORD finished speaking to Moses on Mount Sinai, he gave him the two tablets of the covenant law, the tablets of stone _____ by the _____ of God. **(NIV)**

The Ten Commandments were the ultimate standard for those who followed the law of Moses. And let's not forget that one of those commandments was "Thou shalt not commit adultery," the one that the accusers were supposedly so incensed that this woman had broken. That law was written in the first place by the very finger of God on stone tablets. That finger was now before them wearing human flesh and tracing in the dirt.

Another time the Bible speaks of God writing is in the book of Jeremiah. This time the law God promised to write wouldn't be inscribed on stone tablets or even a dirt floor:

Reread Jeremiah 31:33 and fill in the blanks below:

*"This is the covenant I will make with the people of Israel
   after that time," declares the* LORD.
"I will put my law in their _____
   *and write it on their*_____.
*I will be their God,
   and they will be my people."* **(NIV)**

God wants us to know that the laws He gave us weren't just for external consideration. He doesn't want us to keep His commands out of duty or obligation but because the desire to obey is written on our hearts out of love for Him. He doesn't want His people to use the law as a weapon of judgment, raising it over our heads like a stone to throw and hurt people when they break it. God's hope is that His desires would become our desires. He wants not just a set of rules but a relationship.

How would you explain the difference between following the commands of God written on stone tablets (Exodus 31:18) and having those laws written on your own heart (Jeremiah 31:33)? Your outward actions might be the same, so what would be different?

In Scripture, God uses the metaphors of different kinds of relationships to explain who He is and how He relates to us: King and subject, Father and child, Shepherd and sheep. One of those relationships that really speaks to the heart of God for His people is the bond of Groom to bride, Husband to wife.

Read these Scriptures about the relationship between Jesus and the church. Next to each, write a few words describing what the verses say about that relationship.

Ephesians 5:25-27

> God's hope is that His desires would become our desires. He wants not just a set of rules but a relationship.

Ephesians 5:31-33

Revelation 19:7-9

Why do you think God uses the imagery of Jesus as Groom and the church as bride? What might He be trying to tell us about the kind of love He has for us and the kind of relationship He wants with us?

One of my favorite privileges as a pastor is to perform weddings. I love standing next to the groom as the back doors of the church open and the bride is revealed. I love to see his face when he first sees his bride. It is a look of pure delight. The Bible says that is the way God looks at *you*!

A groom doesn't take his marriage vows with misery through gritted teeth. A bride doesn't walk down the aisle with dread of the days ahead of her. They both have joyful expectation. This kind of relationship exists not because of an obligation or a signed piece of paper. It exists out of mutual love. In this kind of relationship, the other person is not a burden, a "ball and chain"; he or she is the light and love of the other's life.

God's law has sometimes been described as a love letter from God because it can help guide and protect our relationship with Him, allowing us to behave on the outside in ways that mirror the love we have for Him on the inside. When we understand our relationship with God in this way, it's not too much of a leap to recognize why, in Scripture, idolatry is often associated with adultery. Turning away from God and seeking other things to worship is equated with cheating on a relationship. It tells us that the core of the Gospel is more than a list of rules; it's the very personal heart of God.

Read Ezekiel 6:9. Why do you think idolatry is compared to spiritual adultery?

In the story of the woman dragged before Jesus for judgment, the men who hauled her there against her will were guilty of a different kind of sin. They were worshipping an idol: the law itself. They cared far more about the law than they did about a relationship with the God behind it. They wanted to use the law to prove they were more holy than those around them. They were more concerned with the law God wrote than the people God loved.

Have you ever been more concerned about what someone did wrong than you were about that person? Describe what you were thinking and feeling at the time.

How might you have handled the situation differently if you had focused more on relationship than on rules?

In the telling of this story of the unnamed woman, the gospel writer never questions that she was guilty of the sin of which she was accused. But just as guilty as the one who was breaking the law were the ones who were using the law to break her. As Jesus stooped and wrote on the ground that day, His message—whatever He might have written—somehow sunk deeper than just the dirt in which He wrote. It cut straight to the hearts of those who were watching and listening.

Take one more look at John 8:7. After Jesus wrote in the dirt the first time, what did He say to the woman's accusers?

Finally, the men who had wielded the law like a weapon, both against the woman and against Jesus, were redirected to look within their own hearts. They stopped looking at her, or at Jesus, and started looking at themselves. And they gave up their quest and began, one by one, to walk away.

God wants our obedience, but even more than that, He wants our hearts. He doesn't want us to treat our relationship with Him like a marriage in which the partners keep their vows out of obligation. He wants us to be deeply and passionately in love with Him, longing to spend time with Him and to share the joy of our love with others.

If you sometimes feel like you've been following God out of obligation or duty, or that the joy of knowing Him has dimmed, you're not alone. All of us have ups and downs in our relationship with God. But you can know today without a doubt that He loves you deeply and personally, that you matter to Him. The God who created you and knows you through and through longs to write His love for you on your heart.

> *"If any one of you is without sin, let him be the first to throw a stone at her."*
> John 8:7

Pray About It

Jesus, Heavenly Bridegroom, help me to fall in love with You all over again. I want my relationship with You to be reflected in my outward obedience, but I also want my actions to flow out of my heart. Come and write Your word on my heart, and help me to love what You love, desire what You desire, and let my will follow Your will. Amen.

Act on It

- On a separate sheet of paper, list a few of the rules of your household. Next to each, write a reason for the rule that benefits relationships between people in your home. Then list some of God's rules for us. Next to each, write a reason for the rule that protects or benefits the relationships between people or their relationship with God.

Day 3: Casting the First Stone

Read God's Word

⁷ When they kept on questioning him, he straightened up and said to them, "If any one of you is without sin, let him be the first to throw a stone at her."

John 8:7

¹ "Do not judge, or you too will be judged. ² For in the same way you judge others, you will be judged, and with the measure you use, it will be measured to you.
³ Why do you look at the speck of sawdust in your brother's eye and pay no attention to the plank in your own eye? ⁴ How can you say to your brother, 'Let me take the speck out of your eye,' when all the time there is a plank in your own eye? ⁵ You hypocrite, first take the plank out of your own eye, and then you will see clearly to remove the speck from your brother's eye."

Matthew 7:1-5

Reflect and Respond

My friend Amanda grew up going to church every time the doors were unlocked. Her family never missed a Sunday unless they were on vacation. She sang in the youth choir and was a leader in her youth group, and her parents taught Sunday school and led many of the ministries. When she graduated, she decided to attend junior college and live at home for a couple of years while working on a nursing degree. No one was surprised that she chose such a selfless profession. Everyone kept telling her they were so proud and had high expectations for her future.

When Amanda found out she was pregnant at age nineteen, one of her first thoughts was "What will everyone think?" Her sense of personal shame was made even stronger by the feeling that she had let so many people down. When she told her parents, they responded with love and tears, promising to stand by her and help her raise the baby. Even so, she couldn't bring herself to go back to church. She was so worried that everyone was talking about her that once the news of her pregnancy was out, she didn't even drive by the church, much less go in or worship. She avoided her friends and community for months, figuring they would judge her for her mistakes.

One day Amanda's mom called from church, saying her car wouldn't start. She asked her to come and pick her up after a meeting. When she got there, Amanda texted her mom to tell her that she was in the parking lot, and her mom texted back, asking her to come in and meet her inside. Taking a deep breath, Amanda walked through the doors of the church that had once been a second home to her. As she waddled her eight-months-pregnant frame down the hallway, so many memories came flooding back. By the time she pushed open the door of the fellowship hall, she was almost in tears. She was confused when the scene she walked in on wasn't a meeting but a baby shower. "Surprise!" the women of the church shouted, gathering around to hug her and fawn over her with compliments and questions about her plans for the new baby. Amanda blushed, then cried, then sat down and had a piece of cake. She felt like she had come home.

I'm thankful that Amanda was mistaken about her church family's reaction. She expected judgment but received welcome with open arms. But I don't wonder where her worries came from. I'm afraid there are lots of reasons she might have expected a harsh reaction from God's people. We haven't always been so gracious.

The woman dragged into the Temple that day with Jesus was put in that precarious position not by troublemakers off the street but by religious insiders. When she was at her most vulnerable, it was followers of God who wounded her with words and actions of judgment. In their effort to take care that God's laws were followed, they had forgotten to take care not to hurt God's children.

Whatever He was writing on the ground that day, Jesus was a man of few words in this story. Many rabbis might have taken the opportunity to give a treatise on the laws. Rabbis (both past and present) have filled whole books with teachings expounding on just one law. Jesus could have given a lengthy lecture, either to the accusers or to the accused. He chose, instead, to speak only two brief responses. Let's look at the first of those.

Reread John 8:7 and fill in the blanks:

"If any one of you is _____ _____, let him be the first to throw a stone at her." **(NIV)**

The accusers in this story were on the attack, advancing in their moral assault of this woman and closing in on Jesus with an ethical trap, but Jesus, with just one sentence, stopped them in their tracks. Instead of looking at the sins of others, He told them, take a look inside yourself. The question was not *What sin do you find in her?* but *What sin do you find in your own heart?*

When these men, so bold in their accusations, turned their judging eyes on themselves, they became all too aware that none of them (and none of us, for that matter) lives up to the standard of sinlessness Jesus was holding up here. The only one in that crowd who was without sin was the One offering that challenge, and He wasn't picking up any stones.

Jesus didn't condemn the sinner standing before him. He didn't even condemn the other sinners standing there. He had patience and compassion for both the accused and her accusers.

"He who is without sin among you, let him throw the first stone at her" (John 8:7 WEB). I don't have statistics to prove it, but it's my bet that this is one of the most well-known verses in the Bible. I've even heard it quoted by people who don't know much about the Bible at all. They use it to defend themselves when they feel someone is judging them. I'm afraid they also quote it because they feel they have to defend themselves against Christians.

Though we don't pick up rocks to throw at people who have done wrong, we do hurl critical words. We fling disapproving looks. We lob rumors and gossip, even when they are disguised as concern or even as prayer requests.

Reread Matthew 7:1-5. When was the last time you found yourself trying to pick a speck out of someone else's eye? Are there "specks" that bother you more than others—ones you find yourself frequently judging?

Jesus knew that in order to feel better about ourselves, we would be tempted to ignore our own shortcomings and point our fingers at other people. Their sins seem so much bigger, but in reality they're just more visible while ours stay hidden away in our hearts.

Read Luke 18:9-14 and answer the following questions:

What did the Pharisee thank God for? Where was he pointing his finger to point out sin?

What did the tax collector focus on? Where was he pointing his finger to point out sin?

Which man was more likely to encounter God's grace? Why?

When we talk about sin but don't want to sound judgmental, we often use the phrase "Love the sinner, hate the sin." That phrase is filled with good intentions, but it's still a symptom of our outward focus when it comes to sin. How often have you heard anyone say, "God hates sin. And God hates *my* sin! He hates my greed, my selfishness, my lust, my unforgiveness, my jealousy, my critical nature"?

The story of the unnamed woman shows us that God does want us to be on the lookout for sin, but the place He wants us to look is within ourselves. When we do, we will always find room for improvement. It also shows us how to look within the heart of God and find compassion and grace. This helps us to keep from beating ourselves up about our past mistakes.

The intersection of those two hearts laid bare—our own heart marred by sin and the heart of Jesus, sinless and ready to forgive—is a beautiful place. Honesty about our own need for God's powerful and undeserved grace is the only thing that will bring us to confession, which pushes out sin and brings about a vacuum to be filled with forgiveness.

Read John 8:31-36. To what did Jesus say we are slaves (v. 34)?

Did Jesus' listeners recognize that they needed to be free from slavery?

> Honesty about our own need for God's powerful and undeserved grace is the only thing that will bring us to confession, which pushes out sin and brings about a vacuum to be filled with forgiveness.

193

When Jesus said that the truth will set us free, He wasn't referring to a mystical or philosophical truth. The truth He was talking about was in the context of a conversation about our own sinful actions and our slavery to them. A continual focus on the sins of others is hurtful not only to them but also to us, because it puts blinders on our eyes and keeps us from seeing the truth about ourselves. And recognition of that truth is the only thing that will drive us to confession and forgiveness, the true place of freedom.

I met Amanda and became her friend and her pastor years after the surprise baby shower. She told me that story one day as we sat at a church potluck dinner. As we talked, her five-year-old son, Conner, ran circles around that same fellowship hall where the shower had been held. He was as happy and energetic as any five-year-old, stopping to grab a bite off his mom's plate, to get a quick hug from his grandparents, to be tickled by the dad in the family at the table on one side of us, and to exchange a joke with the kids at the table on the other side. All the time he was unaware of the grace running as a current through that room: the grace that was a gift to his mother and now to him as well; the gift of a family of faith that had refused to point a finger but instead welcomed with open arms.

When have you received a gift of grace, rather than a pointing finger?

When Jesus asked for the person without sin in the crowd of accusers to identify himself, no hand went up. That's still true today, isn't it? You and I both know that if we suppress the temptation to keep score in other people's lives long enough to look carefully at our own, we will find a record that is far from perfect. But the good news is that the one sinless heart in the crowd, the heart of Christ, is not one that throws stones at our sin. While others hurl judgment, He offers grace. If you'll let that simple truth sink in, it will dramatically change the way you see others—and yourself.

Pray About It

Loving God, show me the areas where I am tempted to point a finger at others. Give me new eyes to see them the way You see them, and to react to their mistakes with Your grace and mercy. When You give me the gift of being convicted for my own sins, help me to look on my heart with the same gentleness Jesus had for the unnamed woman. Teach me to put down the stones I throw at others and the ones I throw at myself. Make me a part of shaping Your church as a place of welcome and forgiveness. Amen.

Act on It

- Can you think of someone whose mistakes have made her or him feel like an outsider from God's people? Think of a way you can tangibly express your acceptance by reaching out to this person this week.

Day 4: Grace and Truth

Read God's Word

[10] *When Jesus had raised Himself up and saw no one but the woman, He said to her, "Woman, where are those accusers of yours? Has no one condemned you?"* [11] *She said, "No one, Lord." And Jesus said to her, "Neither do I condemn you; go and sin no more."*

John 8:10-11 NKJV

[14] *The Word became flesh and made his dwelling among us. We have seen his glory, the glory of the One and Only, who came from the Father, full of grace and truth.*

John 1:14

Reflect and Respond

Some people say you should quit while you're ahead. End on a high note. Jesus said, "He who is without sin among you, let him throw the first stone at her" (John 8:7 WEB). He could have easily stopped right there. With that one statement, Jesus defended the woman and diffused the conflict. He was now the hero of the story. Why not just stop there?

The unnamed woman had been vindicated against her enemies. The men who seemed so powerful and angry slinked away, licking the wounds of their own sin. What a great ending!

Except for one thing. The woman was still waiting on Jesus. He had said what He needed to say as a closing argument to her accusers, but she was still waiting

Kindness / Jesus - Perfect / Blend of Both

Jesus' entire life was a balance of offering people grace and telling people the truth.

on a verdict. She wanted to know: *What does He have to say to me?* This teacher had told those gathered to look into their own hearts to see if they were sinless. Clearly, she was not. So what would He have to say to her?

Reread John 8:10-11. What did Jesus tell her in verse 11?

In that moment, Jesus offered her release and responsibility. His statements strike such a delicate balance. First He forgave her; then He set her on a new course in life. He gave her freedom from the past and a new path for the future, all in just two short phrases.

"In the beginning was the Word, and the Word was with God, and the Word was God" (John 1:1). The Gospel of John introduces Jesus with a preamble that is pure poetry. It weaves a picture of Jesus that touches both heart and mind before launching into the stories of His life and ministry. One sentence especially captures the tension of the two phrases this story holds in balance.

Reread John 1:14 and fill in the blanks:

"We have seen his glory, the glory of the one and only Son, who came from the Father, full of grace and truth." **(NIV)**

No two words better sum up Jesus' ministry. His entire life was a balance of offering people grace and telling people the truth. Grace without truth means that we'll fall for anything, even while being compassionate. The truth without grace makes us hard and unforgiving, even when we're right.

If Jesus had left her with that first statement, "Neither do I condemn you," she would've walked away free, but she probably would have walked right back into her life of sin. Yet He didn't stop there. Instead, He gave her a gentle command: "Go and sin no more" (John 8:11 NKJV). That phrase isn't quoted nearly as often as the verse we looked at yesterday: "He who is without sin among you, let him throw the first stone at her" (John 8:7 WEB). It's a lot less popular—harder to say and harder to swallow. It says, *When you look inside and recognize your own sin, you need to do something about it.*

Jesus could have comforted her with a "There, there" and sent her on her way. He could have said, "Go, and be yourself; you're OK just the way you are"; "Go, and continue your relationship—you can't help who you love. All love is OK in my eyes"; "Go and enjoy yourself, you deserve to have a little fun." Instead, He said: "Go and sin no more" (John 8:11 NKJV).

"Sin no more" means God wants a better life for us than the one we've been leading. It means we have the responsibility to deal with our own impulses,

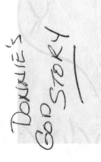

Donnie's God Story

desires, and temptations. It means not only that Jesus wants to forgive us and set us free from our pasts but also that He wants that freedom to stretch into our futures as well. He doesn't want us to continue on the same path and be damaged by the same mistakes over and over again. He wants to eradicate sin from its iron grip on our lives.

Why does God want to free us from sin? Because of His love for us. Just like a parent trying to protect children from choices that can hurt them, God will do anything to protect us from the damaging presence of sin in our lives. Because sin hurts us so badly, it is God's enemy.

What metaphor is used in each of these passages to describe sin?

Psalm 38:4

Isaiah 1:6

Isaiah 1:18

Matthew 6:12

2 Corinthians 7:1

1 John 1:5-6

The woman caught in adultery was a child of God. Jesus loved her and wanted for her a life of wholeness—one she could be proud of. He wanted to protect her from the damage her accusers were trying to inflict, but He also wanted to stop the damage she was inflicting on herself.

Not only did this woman experience the compassion and comfort of Jesus; she experienced conviction as well. Conviction is recognition of your own sin, and it humbles you and moves you to change. Let's talk a little more about the word *conviction*, because when people first experience the awareness of their own sin, they have trouble distinguishing conviction from something else— condemnation.

Conviction is the internalized voice of God, affirming our worth, gently calling us to a life better than our own impulses and offering us a chance to change.

Condemnation is the internalized voices of others that have called us broken and worthless. It calls out the nicknames of our past based on our worst actions and impulses. It's a voice that condemns us to fail over and over again.

When was a time you experienced conviction?

When have you heard an inner voice of condemnation?

Have you ever struggled to tell the difference between the two?

Conviction is an awareness that offers us a chance to change with God's help. Condemnation is a voice that says: you will never change. One is the voice of God. The other is never, ever the voice of God.

Two verses are essential in understanding where God stands on the topic of condemnation. The first follows the most famous passage of Scripture in the entire Bible. Most people know John 3:16, but how often do we quote the verse that follows?

Read John 3:17 and write it below:

Romans 8:1 also reminds us that those of us who know Christ will not receive condemnation from Him. Write the words of that verse here:

How can these two verses help you respond when you hear the voice of condemnation in your life?

A friend's five-year-old came home from school one day and told her dad that the bus driver had used the "S word" on the bus that morning. The dad was furious. How dare someone entrusted with the care of young children use such horrible language! The next morning there he was at the bus stop, holding his daughter's hand and waiting for a chance to give that driver a piece of his mind. As the bus rounded the corner, he reconsidered for a moment, leaned down, and asked his little girl: "Honey, just what did the bus driver say yesterday?"

"You know, daddy. The 'S word'—the bad one." And then whispering, she added, "Shut up."

If you're hearing the voice of condemnation, the one that tells you you'll never be good enough, never change, never be acceptable to God, then it's time to tell it to *shut up!* Because this voice, which often masquerades as the voice of God, is an insidious trick. It drives you farther from the Father, who offers forgiveness for free when we simply recognize our need for Him.

But if you're hearing a voice of conviction, the one that gently corrects, invites you to change, and whispers that there's a path better than the one you're headed down, then continue to *listen up.* God doesn't point out sin because He's against you. He is for you and wants to help you change for the better.

There is no place for the voice of condemnation in a Christian's life. The Bible is clear on that point. The Son of God did not come into this world to condemn. There is now, therefore, *no* condemnation. God doesn't want us to stay captive to our sin that separates us from Him, but neither does He want us captive to a voice that separates us from Him by telling us we don't deserve His forgiveness and grace—or that we're not capable of being better than we have been in the past. That voice is a lie.

When we look at Jesus' interaction with the woman caught in adultery, we don't find even a hint of condemnation. What we do find is an offer to change with His help, an offer at a life that won't keep damaging her, an offer to stop being branded by her past. Jesus didn't want her to be known for the rest of her life as the woman caught in adultery. He wanted to free her from the voice of condemnation and free her from the path that held her captive in the past.

I've always felt a little frustrated that, like in many other narratives of Jesus' encounters in Scripture, we don't know the end of this woman's story. We don't know if she took Jesus up on his offer of a new life. Sometimes, though, I think stories like this are open ended so that we can imagine the ending ourselves. Envisioning her ending helps us, in a way, to ask what we want our own endings to be.

> God doesn't point out sin because He's against you. He is for you and wants to help you change for the better.

Imagine what happened in her life if she accepted Jesus' command to "Go and sin no more." How would her life be different? How would she feel?

Now imagine if she didn't follow Jesus' words. What would her life be like? How would she feel?

What do you want the ending of your own story to be like? Have you accepted God's free gift of grace? Are you listening for His voice of truth?

I wonder if you've ever felt the crushing weight of condemnation in your own life. Have you ever felt stuck in a rut of your own behavior or trapped by the mistakes of your past? The story of the unnamed woman is a gift for those of us who long to lead different lives with God's help. It unveils the beautiful balance Jesus achieves between releasing us from condemnation and offering us responsibility and freedom to choose a different future. That offer stands open for you today!

Pray About It

Jesus, You are so good to offer us freedom. Thank You for the freedom from the condemning voices of others and even the condemning voice that often sounds inside of our heads. Thank You, also, for offering us freedom from our past sins by calling us to "Go and sin no more." If there is anything in my life that is keeping me from You through the deception of sin, please bring me the gift of conviction and the desire and strength to offer that sin to You for forgiveness and change. Let me speak words of compassion and not condemnation over those You love, including myself. Amen.

Act on It

- Identify any weight of condemnation in your own life and surrender it to God today in a time of prayer. Accept Jesus' forgiveness and ask Him to give you the power to change.

Day 5: First-Name Basis

Read God's Word

¹⁸ This is how the birth of Jesus Christ came about: His mother Mary was pledged to be married to Joseph, but before they came together, she was found to be with child through the Holy Spirit. ¹⁹ Because Joseph her husband was a righteous man and did not want to expose her to public disgrace, he had in mind to divorce her quietly.

²⁰ But after he had considered this, an angel of the Lord appeared to him in a dream and said, "Joseph son of David, do not be afraid to take Mary home as your wife, because what is conceived in her is from the Holy Spirit. ²¹ She will give birth to a son, and you are to give him the name Jesus, because he will save his people from their sins."

²² All this took place to fulfill what the Lord had said through the prophet: ²³ "The virgin will be with child and will give birth to a son, and they will call him Immanuel"— which means, "God with us."

²⁴ When Joseph woke up, he did what the angel of the Lord had commanded him and took Mary home as his wife. ²⁵ But he had no union with her until she gave birth to a son. And he gave him the name Jesus.

Matthew 1:18-25

Reflect and Respond

Names are at the center of the sacred ceremonies we hold as Christians. Baptisms, weddings, funerals—all of them are a mix of the sacred and the intimate. Because they're so personal in nature, at the heart of each of them is a person's first name.

"What name is given this child?" "Do you . . . take . . . to be your lawfully wedded husband?" "We are gathered today to remember and give thanks for the life of..."

When I preside over one of these sacred ceremonies, I always make sure I have the first name(s) written in big and bold letters across the top of my notes. Every pastor knows there would be nothing worse than saying the wrong name at a wedding. If you do, the confusion in the eyes of the bride and groom is instant. The glares from the mothers would quickly follow. Even worse would be to say the wrong name at a funeral. You really don't want to make a mistake at the most personal of moments when someone's name is involved.

When Jesus was eight days old, His parents took him to His first religious ceremony, the first of many that He would attend in His lifetime as an observant Jew. But this one was personal. This is where He received His name. The mortality rate for infants in childbirth and shortly after was so great that parents held off giving their boy babies an official name until their circumcision ceremony on their eighth day.

When it came time for Mary and Joseph to announce their tiny baby's name before God and everyone at this ceremony, the name they spoke was probably a shock to many. Some may have even wondered if they made a mistake.

"His name is Jesus."

To those in attendance, this would have been surprising because traditionally firstborn sons were named after their fathers. One reason we know about this custom is that Jesus' slightly older cousin was also given a surprising name.

Read Luke 1:57-66. What did those participating in this child's circumcision and naming ceremony want to name him? Why? What name did he receive?

When we read the story of Jesus' naming, we have the benefit of two pieces of information that most people who were there that day probably did not know. First, we know that Jesus' name was decided before His birth or circumcision day and wasn't chosen by his parents.

In Matthew 1:20-21, who receives news of Jesus' name? Who announces that news? Why is He to be named Jesus?

In Luke 1:26-33, who receives news of Jesus' name? Who announces that news? What else is predicted about Jesus?

Second, we know that despite what people might have expected, Jesus *was* given a first name that reflected His father's identity. It wasn't the name of His earthly adopted father, Joseph, but a name that reflected the character of His Father in heaven.

Let's look at where Jesus' name originated. In Numbers 13, God commanded Moses to send twelve spies into the land of Canaan to see how fruitful it was and how dangerous it might be for God's people to try to move into. One man is chosen from each of the twelve tribes. In Numbers 13:8 we learn the identity of the spy from the tribe of Ephraim: "Hoshea son of Nun."

Only just a few verses later, Hoshea's name is changed, an act that by now should be familiar to us! Just a few verses after he is first mentioned, he is Hoshea no more.

Read Numbers 13:16. What new name is Hoshea given?

This time it's not God who renames someone but a leader, a mentor in faith. Hoshea's name originally meant "Salvation," but Joshua, tweaked by the addition of a new first letter, means "The Lord Is Salvation" or "God Saves." That new letter, *yod*, was meant to point to the name of God revealed to Moses at the burning bush: Jehovah—the name we translate "I AM." By adding that letter it made Hoshea's name—"The Desire for Salvation or Rescue"—a reality. By speaking Joshua's new name, Moses was actually naming aloud the One responsible for His people's rescue: Jehovah. Once, God's people had been so afraid to pronounce that name that they deliberately inserted the wrong consonants for fear that someone would try to say the name of God aloud and by doing so commit blasphemy and incur judgment. Now they were trying to call on that name when they knew they needed saving help, salvation, the most.

As those spies went on their dangerous mission, this one man, Joshua, would prove to be different than the majority of his peers. It's possible that his new name gave him the confidence and insight to see God's hand in every situation, even as dangerous as they found that new land to be. He and one other man, Caleb, would not be afraid of the overwhelming power they found there but would declare that God could give His people victory—that God was powerful enough to save in any situation, just as Joshua's new name announced.

Joshua was right about God's ability to save His people and bring them victoriously into the Promised Land. He became a great leader of God's people, one who went down in history as trusting that "God Saves," just as his name proclaimed.

When Mary and Joseph were called on to name their baby boy, the name they spoke over Him, the name an angel commanded each of them to give Him, was Joshua. God Saves. The Hebrew name Joshua in our Greek translations of the New Testament becomes *Iēsous*, or Jesus. Jesus' first name was Joshua.

In the moment that He received the name Jesus, God the Son became the namesake of God the Father. His name was an echo of the "I AM" (Jehovah) given at the burning bush, that first invitation for God's people to know God's name.

God has a new name that He wants to speak over you. . . . This new name replaces all the unspoken, hurtful labels you've been carrying around and drowns out the inner voices calling you names that are unfit for a child of God.

The truly shocking thing that happened that day is not that Jesus wasn't named Joseph Jr. It's that God Himself offered humanity a chance to be on a first-name basis with Him. Jesus, "God Saves," is His name and His job description all rolled into one. And Jesus fulfilled His name on the cross and through His resurrection when He proved once and for all that God saves.

Through His Son, Jesus, God offers you the chance to approach Him on a first-name basis. That ultimate revelation of who God is and how close to us He desires to be alters our understanding of Him in a spectacular way. What a change from God's people being afraid even to address Him out loud. "Call me Jesus." Thank God He invites us to that kind of closeness with Him.

Names are spoken over us at intimate, holy moments in life because they represent the essence of who we are. And throughout our lives, our names come to embody who we are, both the mundane and sacred parts of our lives. Whether your name is spoken in casual conversation or a sacred rite, it is special because it describes who you are.

God has a new name that He wants to speak over you, one that is different from the name you received at birth, different from the nicknames you've been called or the titles you've received. This new name replaces all the unspoken, hurtful labels you've been carrying around and drowns out the inner voices calling you names that are unfit for a child of God. Scripture tells us this naming ceremony is private and personal.

Read Revelation 2:17. Who will receive a new name, and who will this name be known to?

A new name is a gift. It's a new identity that can come only from knowing the One who created you, the One who knew you before anyone else. Knowing the great I AM has changed who I am. God's revelation of who He is has brought about transformation in my own life. I pray this will be true for you, too. Won't you allow the God of the universe's unconditional love and continual care for you to transform the way you see yourself and what you call yourself? God invites you to a first-name relationship with Him, and He has a beautiful name waiting just for you!

Pray About It

Jesus, we are so grateful that You came near to us, putting on human flesh and taking on a human name so that we can know You. Thank You for Your invitation to approach You on a first-name basis, bearing our hearts and souls to You. As You reveal Yourself to us, we give You ourselves so that we can be transformed. Make us into the beautifully named women of God You long for us to be. In Your holy name we pray. Amen.

Act on It

- Pray about and search for a name that God wants to speak over you. You could find it in one of several ways:
  - Search through the Bible for a verse that really speaks to your heart and what you long for God to do for you. Try to sum that up in one word. Who will you be when God does this for you?
  - Look through a baby name book or website at the meanings of names. Instead of picking a proper name like Abigail, look for a meaning you want to identify with like "Joy of the Father."
  - Choose a name that sums up what you long to become with God's help—what you believe is God's identity for you: Forgiven, Overcomer, Beautiful, Beloved, Cherished, Encourager . . .

Week 6
VIDEO VIEWER GUIDE

Jesus was offering this woman a chance to stop being _branded_ by her _past_.

Our _lives_ are _different_ because Jesus stepped into our _story_.

Safe and Sound—Nautical Terms

Safe meant back _Home_ in dock.

Sound meant the vessel had been _repaired_ from its battle scars.

As God's little _Children_, our wildly _imperfect_ ways haven't affected the way He _sees_ us.

The LORD is my shepherd;

I shall not want.

He makes me to lie down in green pastures;

He leads me beside the still waters.

He restores my soul; He leads me in the paths of righteousness

For _HIS_ _NAME_ _SAKE_.

Psalm 23:1-3 NKJV

Love not Earned!

206

Jessica LaGrone is an acclaimed pastor, teacher, speaker, and writer whose engaging communication style endears her to her audiences. Currently she is Pastor of Worship at The Woodlands United Methodist Church in The Woodlands, Texas, a church with over 8,000 members. In this position she serves as worship architect, planning and developing four of the church's seven weekly worship experiences and working with contractors whose talent in music, media, and preaching build worship services that shine for the glory of God. Her other projects include leading the development of The Woodland UMC's online church initiative and acting as the church's pastoral liaison and chaplain to the Asbury Theological Seminary program. Her popular blog "Reverend Mother" (www.jessicalagrone.com) encompasses her dual roles of pastor and mom. She writes, "This is a blog about having a foot in two worlds, and being imperfect, inadequate, and available to God in both at the same time." Jessica enjoys speaking at retreats and events at churches throughout the United States. She and her husband, Jim, have two young children, Drew and Kate.

Follow Jessica on 🅕 *Facebook,* 🐦 *Twitter,*
and her blog "Reverend Mother,"
jessicalagrone.com.

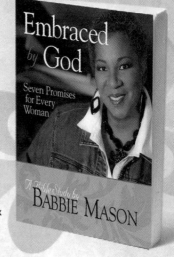